Images of Faith

By the same author:

An Approach to the Metaphysics of Plato

Christ and Apollo

The Image Industries

The Integrating Mind

Images of Hope

Christ and Prometheus: A New Image of the Secular

IMAGES OF FAITH

An Exploration
of the Ironic Imagination

William F. Lynch, S.J.

UNIVERSITY OF NOTRE DAME PRESS
NOTRE DAME   LONDON

Library of Congress Cataloging in Publication Data

Lynch, William F 1908-
  Images of faith.

  1. Faith.   I. Title
BV4637.L94   234'.2   73-11560
ISBN 0-268-00515-X

Contents

Preface

I have always thought that the best way to try to write a book for Everyman—and I share that ambition with most of the writers in the world—is to grasp hold of a question that has long been meaningful and important for yourself; then to objectify it, externalize it into public and human terms, so that, hopefully, it does not remain a private act but becomes a public act in which a good number of the tribe called Everyman will be interested. So it was one thing to write an earlier book to show that faith can let the world, in proper secularity, develop its own independent images of itself and of ourselves; but I was always concerned to know how differently, if at all, faith itself imagined the world; how did faith's images see the world? Was faith a life of the imagination, and in what sense? Thus addling my brain I wrote this book, striving, in the doing, for public action.

It also has a special question behind it which is important but secondary.

The study of the relations between faith and the imagination and, more specifically, between theology and the literary imagination is just about as old as theology and literature themselves. But in the last three decades this relational study has striven, in hundreds of colleges and universities, to reach the status of a special discipline—with success and failure, for good and bad. The effort in these few generations has been so truly broad and the results so mixed that it is time we began making our first appraisal of where we stand at the end of this first epoch. I feel no great immodesty in trying

vii

my own hand at such a task because dozens of other appraisers will appear on the scene and no one will try his hand at anything but a narrow part of the spectrum of the problems involved.

Let me use this preface to express in a broad stroke or two what I think is right and wrong in this new discipline at this moment, hoping like every writer that the whole book will give sense and interstices to the preface. My preface in its small way and my book in its larger way proposes that the greater part of what is right in our new situation (and "discipline") is on the side of literature and the "imagination." It is this right and eminent talent that at any time of reappraisal should be re-balanced as we are always making fresh starts. I believe that the fundamental posture of faith and theology, in an age almost joyously called woe-begone by a great mass of our intellectuals, has been that of a poor relation desperately in need of the support—from the outside—of images, imagination, artists, writers. It is as though faith were a set of beliefs or concepts which today are falling into a wasteland, a "this is the worst of times." The mistake we are making, I think, is in not taking faith itself as a life of the imagination, objective and historical indeed, but a superb life of the imagination for all that. As principal part of my own appraisal I am going to be saying just that.

Faith is a life of the imagination; it is particularly a life of the <u>ironic</u> imagination, and if there is going to be a continuing collaboration between theology and literature it must be a collaboration between imagination and imagination. Anything else will be interesting, occasionally fruitful, but leading into an abyss without true collaboration and often without any real contacts; often

viii

there will be as much of hidden quarrels and misunderstandings as there is of open contact. Only when theology and literature come to have mutual respect for each other, not as sets of standards or morals versus orders and guardians of sensibility, but as vision aiding vision and creativity aiding creativity will the next step in collaboration become possible.

Of course this adds just one more grievous burden to the life of faith and theology. But neither will it make life easier for art and the literary imagination. For if faith too is a life of the imagination, it is only because imagination and the images of faith are compact, as are all our best images, with thought. And if literature is going to collaborate with faith it cannot be in terms of an aesthetic of pure sensibility. There can be no limit to the thought and the thoughts its images must contain. We must return to an older but more burdensome tradition that the poet is a thinker without limit.

Within these two paradoxes collaboration might enter a new phase: Let theology, among the many things that it is, become a set of images of faith and a life of the imagination. Let the poet, always the imag-er, become also the thinker without limit.

The very opposite of all this is said in a book by Erick Havelock called Preface to Plato. *I dearly love Plato, but no one helps Plato by overstating the case for him: by proposing that Greek thought began with Plato and the concept, and that neither faith nor the imagination "thinks." But if faith is a life of the imagination, neglected at its own risk by the guardians of the imagination, and if the poet, the artist, the dramatist, are willing to readopt the names and tasks of thought, then why can we not begin an always new life of collaboration.*

But this is a preface. The first task of a preface is to make an elusive, even a mysterious stab at the subject and intention of the book. The second task is to be thankful. I am most grateful, and not for the first time, for the competence and wisdom of Ann Rice, the editor of this book. If a third time does not occur, it will be my loss. Then there is Thilda Hadjiyanni, citizen of Athens; not even much illness prevented her from finishing the typing of the manuscript. If I return to Athens to see so many other Athenian friends again I would be most grateful of all. It was right that a book on the ironic imagination should have in substance been done where the first great masters of irony taught us the mastery of this extraordinary human gift. There are two other very living students of theology and irony, two Jesuit friends, who helped me more than I can say, George McCauley and George Hunt.

PART ONE
IMAGINING FAITH

1: Faith and the Imagination:

Being an Introductory Chapter

I CALL THIS BOOK *IMAGES OF FAITH* AND I MEAN THE TITLE IN two separate but deeply related senses:

1. The first sense of the title (comprising Part One of the book) is: What are our images of faith? That is to say, how do I imagine faith?

I take this to be a very crucial question. I am firmly convinced that the way we imagine anything (literally, the way we image anything) is precisely what leads to the solution or the creation of a question. In *The Republic* Plato asked the question: Is goodness in itself, without extrinsic advantage and even with disadvantage, worthwhile? And the method of his answer is simply to imagine goodness, to carve out a great image of it. When it is successfully imagined there is no need to say more. The matter is settled. The question vanishes as question. I am proposing that many of our problems with faith and many of its problems and crises and dilemmas in modern theology are caused by the way we imagine faith, that we should therefore re-imagine it.

In my own lesser way I imitated this fundamental method of *The Republic* in a recent book in which I proposed a new image of secularity within which the religious imagination could live and breathe.[1] To my mind the problem was the same. The degraded and demythologized image of secularity that had been created by both the secular and the religious imagination was responsible for most of our difficulties as we tormented ourselves with many of the issues of the sacred and the world. It was necessary to re-imagine the secular. And this I tried to do, with what success I am not the one to say.

Let us begin to do the same thing with faith. One image we have had of faith is that temporally it always follows knowledge and adds to knowledge its own fine images of the universe. We then proceed to agonize over the great modern questions. What does faith add to knowledge? What does faith add to, or how does it help with, experience? What does Christ add to the human? What does Christ add to Heidegger? Laplace, we are reminded, answered Napoleon's question, how does God fit into your hypothesis? by saying: There is no place for God in my hypothesis. John Wisdom questions whether the coming and going of the Great Gardener makes any difference to the garden of the world, or adds to it.[2] Even Dietrich Bonhoeffer comes close to the same images and the same problems. Are not these questions and problems caused in large part by the image of the temporal sequence: knowledge, then faith?

Another image we have of faith is that it has a magnificently vertical but only a vertical life, in God, in the unknowable and the unimaginable. Faith has no body or embodiment or horizontal life. It does not experience the world. It does not create society. Thus we imagine. But why not periodically re-imagine?

*   *   *

2. The second sense of the title Images of Faith (comprising the second and more important part of the book) is: How does faith imagine or experience the world? What are faith's images of the world? Is faith a way of imagining or experiencing the historical and contemporary world? I think it is and I think it must be. (In all simplicity we first imagine faith and then let faith imagine).

Faith is *a form of imagining and experiencing the world.*

My intention is to compose a sketch of the internal relations between faith and the imagination. (Who could do more than a sketch when faced with the vast world that is summarized by this title Images of Faith?)

I use the phrase *internal relations,* and it is very central to my purposes. Now, for a whole generation, we have been passing through the first stages of a new field of work and thought, in which faith and theology, having been told on every side that they are in danger of death or senescence, have been calling on the imaginative help of literature and the arts to restore them to life or youth. My own work has been firmly involved in this collaboration between theology and the arts. But I have one serious methodological proposal for this field of work, and one reason for this study is the wish to project and develop that proposal. I see, happily, that faith has been calling on the life of the imagination, upon literature and art, for help. The methodological supposition has often been: here on the one side is theology and faith, in serious if not desperate trouble; here on the other side, waiting as a frequently sympathetic and potent ally, is the imagination, with its long history of the illumination of the human at its best and worst. Thus we call upon that history, from Greek tragedy to Kafka, to give imaginative light or reinforcement to faith. But what is nearly always omitted as a necessary and colleague half of this new exploration is the study of faith as itself a form of experience and imagination, itself a way of *imagining* and experiencing the world. This is what I mean when I say that my concern in this study is the *internal relations* between faith and the imagination. It makes far from perfect sense to explore external and collaborating relations unless we have a firmer understanding of this internal equation. If we have a better understanding of the latter *we will be in the healthier position of creating a collaboration between imagination and imagination.* And it will mean that faith does not collaborate in the terms of a collapse of its own self-confidence and nerve.

Is faith a colleague imagination, or is it a desiccated beggar in search of help from the artist and the literary imagination? Has it a seeing-power and identity of its own that it is absolutely necessary to imagine and let imagine? Even if we find the need of revitalization or renewal or revival of faith from death itself, it is not a good methodology that the revival or the recovery of identity come from the imagination unless we have first restored faith's own imagination and images. Otherwise faith, and theology with it, loses its nerve and can neither discover nor declare itself. If it reveals its own image, and images, then, knowing its own face, it is ready for collaboration without end. But the best way is a *pari passu* double action of a conversation with itself and a conversation with human culture.

* * *

When I say that faith is a form of imagining *and experiencing* the world, I am also hypothesizing, and I think correctly, that there is an equation between the imagination and experience.

The imagination, and the images it forms, is the mode in which we experience and manage the world. That is not all that it is, as we shall see, but to imagine the world is to experience the world. If faith, therefore, is indeed a way of imagining the world, it is also a way of experiencing the world. I intend to say at length how that is so, and according to what modes and images. Meantime let me refer to the work, almost the totality of the work of John Macmurray, the English philosopher, who has made the most vigorous statement I know of to the effect that faith must suffer catastrophe if not powerfully related to experience. That statement is to be found principally in his books *The Self as Agent, Persons in Relation, Search for Reality in Religion,* and *Interpreting the Universe.*

But let us pause here before we make a serious mistake. For we are in grave danger of falling into a trap when we say that faith must be in vigorous relationship to experience. The trap would be that experience would be thought of as a separate, prior, and independent world and faith would be thought of as an external and later addition, as something that is in the relationship of relevancy to experience. It seems a very impressive statement when it is said so often today that faith must be relevant, but I believe that this is a halfway house, a position that must be bypassed.

To be on the *outside* of experience and relevant to it could be a fate worse than death. We must under no circumstances accept the beautiful but mistaken position of relevancy.

* * *

As for the word *experience,* to understand any single word, phrase or sentence, it is usually necessary to determine the larger vocabulary or world within which it occurs. Thus it is with the phrase "faith as place of imagination and experience." When I use this phrase I am not using the traditional or classical vocabulary which set up certain sharp but necessary distinctions between experience and faith, understanding and faith, science and faith, evidence and faith, imagination and faith. This vocabulary (and the enormous theological structure that went along with it) was created to deal with a set of specific problems, and especially the problem of the relationship and separation of nature and grace. Historically it had become crucially important to maintain a world and a vocabulary in which the supernatural is absolutely superior to every form of human knowledge and experience. This will always be crucial and necessary. But in the meantime other needs have risen for the solution of which this vocabulary may have no special talent. One of these needs is to relate faith to *experience,* but not according to an older and more limited meaning that had been given to the word.

* * *

The form I use in the exploration of my two central questions is a modest imitation of the form of Pascal's *Pensées.* Each unit stands on its own as a unit thought or question or meditation or speculation. Each section or part or half of the book is tied together by a central question or exploration or logic but in a looser and more flexible way than that tight logic which ordinarily binds paragraphs and chapters of a book. This allows for more freedom of speculation and hypothesis. It allows me to do more sudden things, like recommending a very good book. It does not impose on me some dismal sense of the final and the definitive in questions we are only beginning to explore. It does not take away any of my own responsibility but it allows me also to impose responsibility on the reader, responsibility for exploring some suggestion (or not), or even for writing another book on the subject. In addition, the method seems, for me, enjoyable.

*   *   *

The next thing to do is to define the subject again but with a little more light on the meaning and direction of the two senses of Images of Faith.

Our first question is: How shall we imagine faith? What are my images of faith itself? They are of course various but when the time comes I shall develop two images or two facets of an image which I think to be completely central.

The first is an imaging of faith as the most primary, the most elemental force in human nature; it is a force which *precedes* what we ordinarily call knowledge and all the forms of specific knowing; this force is uneducated and needs education; it is educated by knowledge of every kind, by people to every degree, by irony but not by every irony; last of all it is formed and educated by Christ. I am myself principally concerned with its education by irony, by the ironic imagination, and by the irony of Christ. I reverse the sequence to: faith-knowledge.

It is in this powerful, turbulent, primal form that we must first image faith.

*   *   *

I will often be using the word *faith* in a specifically religious sense but the first understanding of it that I am projecting is that of a primal and broad force of belief, promise, and fidelity which—by its presence or absence, by its operation or collapse, by its goodness or fury, by its fidelities or treacheries—shapes (or misshapes) the welfare, shall I say the very existence, of men and women in life and society. This force, and all the powerful experiential elements that belong to it, should be imagined as moving historically into and up to a religious context, especially under the educating action of the promises of God and the reactions of men; but the movement is such that all this broad and primal life remains integral to religious faith as its body. It is of this broad and primal power that I shall be speaking first, and I shall be doing it in terms of such great metaphors as mother and child, man and wife, Medea, and particularly Dionysus. Above all, I shall be first thinking of it as not yet educated by irony. Dionysus represents an ecstatic stage of faith that is turning toward God but is as yet completely unironic. The irony of Christ will be the peak of educated faith. In turn, that peak is not only transcendental; it nurses the whole horizontal life of faith, especially the poor.

I should only add that by primal faith—and revelation—I do not mean that first religious faith which was given to man before he fell into some earthshaking sin and before he fell under the sense of some curse. That first age does not belong to the province of this book. What I meditate and speculate upon are all the primal and primitive forms of faith which then emerged and still emerge in the affairs of individuals and nations. However, I shall not neglect that curse but shall devote a whole section to it. For it occupies a mysterious place in our national life. In what form it should appear among us, in its consequences, in our death, it is denied. And where it is not, where it should no longer hold us, for there is no longer a curse, it keeps a terrible grip upon us. Such images of the curse impose their guilt upon our personal lives; they also affect the political life of the nation more than do national elections. Perhaps we can say that they are images of a primal faith out of which individuals and nations still try to raise themselves.

*   *   *

In theological studies we have always thought of faith as a final superb gift of God and a form of divine knowledge, prefaced in many ways by rationality but giving a later, a more ultimate view of the universe than knowledge. This may be true chronologically of the final forms that Christianity gives to faith, but if we let the picture go at that we would be distorting faith and would finally be distorting Christian faith itself. This picture, left to itself, tends to make faith a later addition, even if a refinement, to knowledge, and to separate faith from knowledge. And I repeat that it also tends to raise all those problems with which modern theology

has been preoccupied: What does faith add to knowledge, what does Christ add to the idea of man, what
does Christ add to Heidegger? We must get out of this
cul-de-sac by changing our temporal image of faith.
Faith comes first.

There is room in theology for hypothesis and speculation if the hypothesis and speculation are then seriously
explored. In this case let us explore the hypothesis that
the time picture of faith should be largely reversed. Let
faith not be an old man attached at a later date to
human culture and knowledge. Let it be present at and
carved as central force into the very birth of man. If he
cannot immediately believe someone he is immediately
lost. This can be and has been established clinically for
childhood, and I shall have more to say about it when I
come, in the last and most important part of this book,
to study the rhythm, the different ways, in which faith
imagines the world according to the various stages of
human life. It will start as a mighty torrent; knowledge
and science will be some of its food. Christ will be its
final food. Thus, we do not ask, what does Christ
contribute to knowledge? but what does he contribute
to faith?

*   *   *

Another facet of my image of faith, another way of
imagining (and experiencing) it will be to see it as
existing not only in a vertical relationship with God and
the unknowable but also as horizontally alive, in the
most imaginable way, in various forms of "embodiment"—individual, historical, social, political—to such
an extent that it creates the very heart and core of
human existence and human society.

Faith, I repeat, has a horizontal as well as a vertical life; it has a body; indeed it has many bodies. (I am not here talking of the "mystical body" of the Church, though later I will not exclude that meaning as one of the profound embodiments of faith.) And because faith is embodied it is imaginable. Above, all, it is so embodied in the political order that it is the very creating substance and life of the political order. It is not just "relevant"; the truth is that it is the thing itself. It enters so deeply and visibly into the political order that its capacity to be imagined or experienced will be seen to be not a problem but a truism. As its presence is the very life of the political order, so its absence is its death. Thucydides saw how true this was and has given us his immortal and frightening picture of the collapse and corruption of faith among the Greeks at Corcyra. Now among us, for ten long years, our own country claimed the Vietnam War as our point of crisis. But I did not and do not believe this. I think that a far worse crisis was and is going on, the true war, which is such a collapse of faith between the two major culture classes as has hardly every occurred so sharply in our history. These two groups are the middle class on the one hand and, on the other, the intellectual-academic culture. I shall be speaking of *this* collapse of faith at greater length.

*   *   *

But because for me the more crucial part of my study is concerned with the second sense of my title Images of Faith, with faith's images of the world, I will spend the remaining units of this introduction in trying to express in some highly compressed way what I mean by it. Can faith possibly "imagine" or "experience" the world? If so how?

I want to have outlined four things about the Hebraic-Christian faith as prime imaginer of the world.

1. It is a paradigm within which we experience or imagine the world.

2. It is not a passive but a creative paradigm, one which activates the imagination.

3. It is a moving paradigm which will not be understood until it has moved through all the stages of the life of man and, in the same act, all the stages of the life of Christ.

4. It is an ironic paradigm. This is so important that I have chosen irony, the ironic imagination, the irony of faith, the irony of Christ, as the real subject of this book.

I shall be talking at great length about irony, ironic images, the ironic image of faith, the irony of Christ, in this book. Let me not hesitate to say immediately that the irony we will be talking about so much is a distinctive paradigm or patterning of facts, a re-composing in which a fact (e.g., "having nothing") is seen within the creative presence of a contrary ("and possessing all things"). This is a simple form of irony but it does not go wrong. A later chapter will examine the permanent features of irony in faith, and a final section will watch irony grow as it moves, in the one act, through all the stages of human life and all the stages of the life of Christ, until it reaches its most powerful moment (and opposite) in death.

*   *   *

A paradigm. There seems to be a growing conviction among scientists that while each unit fact does or can have its own unique life, there remains an extraordinary need of some kind of previous general visual-conceptual experience if the new fact is to be found or known or identified. Without this pre-existing paradigm one could not discover a fact, one could not have experience even in the simplest sense of that word. While we are not yet further analyzing what this means, we must remember that faith is such a paradigm.

A book that deals most helpfully with our present problem is *The Structure of Scientific Revolutions* by Thomas S. Kuhn.[3] Another, sharper in language and example, is *Patterns of Discovery* by Norwood Russell Hanson. (One of Hanson's first exemplary questions is: "Let us consider Johannes Kepler: imagine him on a hill watching the dawn. With him is Tycho Brahe. Kepler regarded the sun as fixed; it was the earth that moved. But Tycho followed Ptolemy and Aristotle in this much at least: the earth was fixed and all other celestial bodies moved around it. Do Kepler and Tycho see the same thing in the east at dawn?")[4]

*   *   *

Now what, more fully, do we mean when we say there is no experiencing or imagining a fact without a paradigm, hypothesis, or expectation?

1. It is fascinating to see how separate and remote from each other our understandings of the words *experiencing* and *imagining* had become in our culture and how much they now begin to approach each other.

Experience had come to be thought of as our world of contact with pure fact, a world of pure observation of established fact, absolutely present or given before all interpretations, hypothesis, theory, imagining, believing—a world belonging to pure observers of pure facts that remained the same no matter what. For Hume, Mill, and Russell the mind was first of all a bucket, an empty receptacle for the reception and observation of *given* facts. If this were the case, then neither thought nor faith nor imagination could be anything but a later addition to, and interpreter of, fact and experience. Imagination, on the other hand, was another world, a world beginning, pejoratively, where "fact" ended. At best, imagination created another universe to live and breathe in when "facts" became unsatisfactory. Fact, together with that experience by which we contacted fact (remote from theory, imagination, or faith), had become crown prince. The fact was, according to the small boy talking about the sting of a bee, that the stinger was actually very small and the rest was imagination. The two worlds of experience and imagination had become separated.

2. But today one serious figure after another is proposing the opposite. They tell us that one cannot begin to discover a fact or make an observation without a set of expectations, without a hypothesis; we search the world around us for what will verify or falsify the expectations or hypothesis. This way of doing things is not the result of a decision but is built into the human organism; neither should it be thought of as subjectivity, but as a new and more human form of objectivity. But so close is the marriage of thought and fact that if a new theory emerges we alter both the original concepts and the original "facts." There is not even such a thing as pure appearances (the first look of things before we think or imagine or believe). We have already given a structure, from the very first, to appearances. Where we

cannot do this in some fundamental way, where we cannot give fundamental organization to appearance, the result is the terrifying escalation of insecurity and even mental illness.

Faith, I am suggesting, has a similar relationship to the world; it provides a structure or a context. It is a way of experiencing and imagining the world; or it is a world within which we experience or imagine. It composes it or, if you will, it recomposes the world according to its terms. For example, the beatitudes totally recompose ordinary appearance. To believe that the poor are *blessed* puts an entirely different light on things.

*   *   *

Conversion of point of view, the very possibility of seeing or experiencing things differently, implies that we can change and can see things differently; it implies change is not an enemy or a threat but a possibility of life and of salvation itself. We know clinically that the frequent effect of severe early traumatic experience in life is a fixation in this experience, a constant compulsive return to it in order to try to work it out and move out of it. The sense of impossibility of change or escape or movement into a new point of view produces something akin to despair. Real change produces the opposite. The possibility of change is identical with hope itself. Where there is no hope, or very little, it is because the imagination is literally stuck or trapped and cannot change its images.

If the images seem "not important," it is because we take them for granted. We do not reflect on how much they *think,* how much is in them.

Just as there is no such thing as a pure fact or experience, there is no such thing as a pure image. The whole of us gets into the images.

Our basic images are also filled with imagining and thinking. Thus with the images of man, woman, child, death, birth, thing, that thing, that fellow, friend, enemy, we, they, me, child, that look, that moment.

There is the enormous mathematical system with which a modern scientist approaches a supposedly pure fact. Or the enormous content of the image which a parent has of his child.

I once expressed the thought to three friends as we had dinner together: There is no such thing as a pure fact. One answered sharply: Of course there is; we four are *here.* My triumph (in asking, "but what does *here* mean?") was easy in the given case, and obvious in the light of the endless imagining in the eye of my friend who had waited for fifty years to get to that lovely restaurant in Athens, the center of his world.

*   *   *

Coleridge and his followers—including Croce and Collingwood—still used the word *imagination* to designate a single faculty. Today we think less and less of it in these special and often mystical terms. My own fundamental understanding of it is that the imagination refers to the total resources in us which go into the making of our images of the world. It is, therefore, all the faculties of man, all his resources, not only his seeing and hearing and touching but also his history, his education, his feelings, his wishes, his love, hate, faith and unfaith, insofar as they all go into the making of his images of the world. The simplest of our images, therefore, are quite complicated, and nothing comes nearer to defining human beings than their images of the world—than, shall we not then say, their imaginations. By what and for what shall we be judged more than by and for our images? For can we not conclude, if all that I have just said is true, that we are much more responsible for the shape of our images than is customarily assumed? Or cannot a whole social group be responsible for its escalation of the images of another group? We shall see many times that there is no such thing as a simple or pure image, untouched by abstraction or thought or context or shaping or faith.

*   *   *

I take the word *paradigm* as a very provisional word, not trusting it too much, and the remainder of this introduction is an attempt to overcome some of its limitations. Unhappily, it has some of the connotations of being a rigid and final form, an archetype for the classification and immobilizing of experience and life. Again it sounds as though I am trying to place a previously existing experience within a Christian category.

*   *   *

Faith is an activating paradigm. It generates active imagining.

In the case of the artist, not all the images he creates are his own work; they are as much the images he makes us form ourselves, and he is a better artist if he makes us thus active, if, that is, he makes us do half the work. If he does not make us imagine and form (or re-form) our own image as he gives his, then his own work tends to render us helpless. We are simply under extreme bombardment. But the true artist, being an active imaginer himself, wishes to make active imaginers out of us; he does not wish to form all the images (neither do the images of faith).

This must be particularly true of the art of the dramatic imagination. For the dramatic imagination must not so much move us as make us move from one step of insight to another, and it is ourselves as spectators who must get halfway ahead of the game. When Oedipus, who has relentlessly pursued the quest for what will turn out to be his terrible identity, comes to the final moment and hears the shepherd say "I am upon the dreadful brink of speech," and when he responds "and I of hearing," it is at such a point, and at thousands of points like it in the history of the dramatic imagination, that we ourselves come to the dreadful brink of imagining. The images of all the things now to be recognized (re-cognized) or re-shaped flood in upon us without a further word from the artist. The walls of non-imagining are down. As the imagination moves out of the present into the future it is called upon to re-pattern everything that has occurred in the past of the play. And we do it, not Sophocles.

Part of the implicit charge of Dostoevski's Grand Inquisitor against Christ is that he *did not* lead the imagination by assault into immobility and slavery. What Christ did was to create in his own person a permanent propaedeutic for the original and active imagining of men in every generation.

*   *   *

What happens when the imagination is too much assaulted by an omnipotent moment of art or by images that simply bruise it is that we simply refuse to form images or cannot. The walls go up again; the activity stops.

When the walls are down, when the block is gone, when the imagination is free, the images do indeed rush in upon us, but they are also our own, a very mountain in labor trying to come to grips with so great a perception. Within a single moment there is space and time enough for wave after wave of awareness, imagining, thinking, and for a beginning of a review (re-view) of the irony of it all: that this man Oedipus who had all the time been searching for a criminal and a source of national pollution had all the time been searching for himself. But that famous moment is only a part of the new picture. Now it is as though a complete playback (re-play) had been caused by the simple image of the king and the peasant, with the final clue confronting each, the one about to speak, the other about to hear. Now *everything* that had occurred in the play should come rushing back, crowding into the present in this new light. We watch Oedipus imagine everything anew. The peasant who had in pity saved Oedipus as a child sees how ironic was his pity. The fatal garrulity of the second peasant and messenger from Corinth is seen for what it truly was. And so with the boasting of the wife-mother Jocasta against all oracles and gods. The back and forth between past, present, and future seems endless.

But it is we who did it, with help. Sartre rightly describes reading as directed creativity. The recorded

Hebraic-Christian images of faith act in the same way. They do not try to destroy the imagination but give it freedom and life.

*   *   *

I make brief note of some initial materials for the directed and directing imagining of faith. We read the great events of the book of Exodus, the sufferings in Egypt, the education and leadership of Moses, the leading of the people out of Egypt, Israel in the desert, the covenant and decalogue. We then turn to Deuteronomy to hear Moses remind the people of everything and to recompose a new present in terms of the past. The present is always new and unexpected; the event is never exactly repeated; the present is always one's own; faith no more than Sophocles treats us as children; it demands active imagining; it is always asking us to put the expected (of the promises of God) together with the historical forms of the unexpected.

The imagination must meet event after event, disaster after disaster, blessing after blessing. The history in the book of Nehemiah (2 Esdras) is different, but with the help of the prophet the imagination finally succeeds in putting together the old and the new story and in moving from darkness into light. But it is not simply a matter of reducing present history to past event, or even of understanding a past revelation better; the new has its own insight; Jeremiah leads into a deeper interiority; the revelation is continuing; one must be perpetually on the watch for the new; the body of sensibility is always building; the Spirit is always breathing; there is always need for discernment, and for the discernment of spirits; I shall myself be struggling through many pages which shall be trying to discern the differences between many forms of irony, trying to discern which are and which are not images of faith. The Jewish task after Dachau is greater than ever. The task is never done. Neither faith nor history can be reduced to a science. But the images of faith do try to keep moving, in the one action, through the life of Christ and the life of every man, each contributing law and flexibility to the other. So that our paradigm now is not only creative but in motion.

*   *   *

A moving paradigm. In the last and longest part of this study, I try to "dramatize" the images of faith by watching them move through the rhythm, the stages, the temporal form of human life. For the sake of continuity and, hopefully, of development, I think that if there is any one consistent theme in my own explorations of the life of the imagination over the years it is this: the imagination, if it is to get anywhere in insight, understanding, or vision, must progressively *move through* the finite, the detail, the definite, the phases, the time, the stages of the human and of human life. Faith must make the same patient movement.

Man is temporally built to get somewhere; that is especially true of his imagination, which gets somewhere precisely by this movement through human time and through all of the human. Let us follow this clue in the case of faith.

It is by no capricious or artificial decision that the great body of the images of faith, as we have known them historically and as a developed body of sensibility, have moved, in one and the same act, through the stages of the life of man and the stages of the life of Christ.

There is the movement of Christ, in the history of painting and sculpture, through all the stages of the human. Thus Christic-human life dominates the museums and churches of the West. There is the annual movement of Christ through life in the liturgy (and in the public prayer of the Divine Office). In ascetical literature there are all those documents which lead the soul in a spiritual retreat and set of meditations through the detail of the life of Christ; as this writer is a Jesuit it will be understandable if he should be preoccupied in a special way with the *Spiritual Exercises* of St. Ignatius, which lead the meditator, over four weeks of meditating four or five times a day, through the detail and length and breadth and shape of the stages of the life of Christ. I have always been convinced that the unique feeling of liberation which seems to be reached at the conclusion of these "exercises" comes largely from that epic sense of the unique growth, rhythm, and amplitude of life as we imagine the Son of Man pass through all its human dimensions. The purely human analogues of all these great Christic marches, with their corresponding liberation of the human spirit, will be found in such temporal and spatial amplitudes as *The Iliad* or *War and Peace*.

*   *   *

Finally, the paradigm is ironic. Then finally, in this introduction, I should like to make an experiment to sharpen the contemporary problem for the imagination as it deals thus temporally again with the stages of man and the stages of Christ. I will turn back to the theater material of the Middle Ages. I will pick out the York cycle Ms. of the great miracle plays. I will take the space to enumerate the single plays produced in the cycle, together with the producing guild, and will call the reader's attention to an inevitable but now disturbing image of faith: of the forty-eight unit plays that run through the history of Christ (passing through the mysteries of man) and the history of the world before and after, from creation to judgment, thirty-seven have to do in one way or other with the life of Christ. Part of the answer may be that, after all, this was the principal subject of all these cycles; but it is also true that this is the way life was then imagined cosmologically: there were a limited set of events before and a limited set of events after; the imagination had no difficulty imagining Christ at the center. Thus:

I.   *The Barkers.*
     The Creation, Fall of Lucifer.

II. *Playsterers.*
     The Creation to the Fifth Day.

III. *Cardmakers.*
     God creates Adam and Eve.

IV. *Fullers.*
     Adam and Eve in the Garden of
     Eden.

V.   *Cowpers.*
     Man's disobedience and Fall.

VI. *Armourers.*
     Adam and Eve driven from Eden.

VII. *Glovers.*
     Sacrificium Cayme et Abell.

XIX.   *Gyrdillers and Naylers.*
         Massacre of the Innocents.

XX.   *Sporiers and Lorimers.*
         Christ with the Doctors in the Temple.

XXI.   *Barbours.*
         Baptism of Jesus.

XXII.   *Smythis.*
         Temptation of Jesus.

XXIII.   *Coriours.*
         The Transfiguration.

XXIV.   *Cappemakers.*
         Woman taken in Adultery. Raising of Lazarus.

XXV.   *Skynners.*
         Entry in Jerusalem.

XXVI.   *Cutteleres.*
         Conspiracy to take Jesus.

XXVII.   *Baxteres.*
         The Last Supper.

XXVIII. *Cordewaners.*
         The Agony and Betrayal.

XXIX.   *Bowers and Flecchers.*
         Peter denies Jesus: Jesus examined by Caiaphas.

XL.	*The Sledmen.* Travellers to Emmaus.
XLI.	*Hatmakers, Masons, and Laborers.* Purification of Mary: Simeon and Anna Prophesy.
XLII.	*Escreueneres.* Incredulity of Thomas.
XLIII.	*Tailoures.* The Ascension.
XLIV.	*Potteres.* Descent of the Holy Spirit.
XLV.	*Draperes.* The Death of Mary.
XLVI.	*Wefferes.* Appearance of our Lady to Thomas.
XLVII.	*Osteleres.* Assumption and Coronation of the Virgin.
XLVIII.	*Merceres.* The Judgement Day.
(Fragment.)	*Inholders.* Coronation of our Lady.[5]

*   *   *

Visually the center (the life of Christ) is not only important; it practically monopolizes the scene.

But now let us watch the image change. One has but to read Stephen Toulmin and June Goodfield's *The Discovery of Time* or the two fascinating books on the emergence of the infinite by Alexander Koyré (*From the Closed World to the Infinite Universe*) and C. F. Von Weizsäcker (*The World View of Physics*) to follow the transformations.[6] The space and the time widen at both ends of the picture. Infinite time, infinite space, endless history, endless change emerge. Visually the great supporting sacred center seems to diminish to the size of a pinpoint.

The temporal vistas occupied now by the story of man and his ancestors become enormous (and these vanish into a smaller line when compared with the billions of light years of astronomic time). A true man emerged in Shensi province, China, nearly three-quarters of a million years ago. Further north, near Peking another man used fire a half million years ago, in the lower Pleistocene age. But we now struggle to trace with increasing accuracy into the hominoid and hominid lines these not yet human lines, these lines of decreasing similarity but lines indeed, through perhaps thirty-six million years of time. And before that there is the staggering time of the universe.[7]

If we were to use one form of irony—this book proposes that there are endless forms and that we are in search of the irony of faith—but if in this case we considered irony to be a mighty demon and a principle of universal negation, we might think of this new world ironizing every limited, definite thing, ironizing it out of existence, dissolving it, dissolving all. Then Yeats's phrase returns to the ear: The center cannot stand.[8] Thus the definite and the infinite become locked in mortal combat. Another way I shall be putting the matter often in the pages ahead of us is that the small human line and the large expanded technological or cosmological line also become locked in new and intense attempts to work out relationship.

I would ask the reader to keep the pair of images in mind as he reads the book: the image from the York Plays and the expanding image of space and time. Every irony deals well or badly with the problem of putting these two images together, that of the small line and that of the large line: I will be especially interested in the way the images of faith and the irony of faith perform this task.

*   *   *

Socrates had his own way of putting the larger and the smaller thing together. He who knows nothing becomes the only man in Athens who is wise. And he who is ugly is the beautiful one. And he dismantles, to his cost, the great wisdoms of the city.

In the *Pensées* Pascal handles the two lines and the two images with incredible insight. First of all, he lets the two things stand together, the misery and the glory of man—thus perhaps becoming the first modern man, for modern man is capable of letting contraries stand together. And part of his insight is that he is not sure if the greatness lies in the misery or the misery in the greatness.

Thomas Mann, who was the great modern ironist, declares the problem of irony to be the most majestic problem of all for the human mind. Those who know him well know how much he has wrestled with every form of the ironic. And one has but to read the mighty introduction to *Joseph and His Brothers* to see how in his mightier and brilliant way he does battle with contending images equivalent to those of the York Plays and the new vast temporal universe. As writer and storyteller Mann plunges with fear into the great abyss of time to discover the definite forms or moments of Joseph, Jacob, Esau, Laban, Leah, Rachel, Dinah, all the sons of Jacob, and many others; every such single point loses its form and dissolves into some older prototype and part of man; the restless writer, like another Jacob, another Israel, moves on and on, dissolving time into timelessness or trying to keep the two together; it is a march of irony itself: "And here indeed our tale issues into mysteries, and our signposts are lost in the endlessness of the past, where every origin betrays itself as but an apparent halt and inconclusive goal. . . ."[9]

Here and now I will only say of Christ that he deepens the problem before he imagines answers of his own. How does he restore power to the single images and the human pinpoints in space? By changing the whole concept of power, by using poverty, tragedy, the curse itself, according to his own irony. But that is a long story, and it will still be a long story when this book is ended. For it involves the whole history of all our struggling to give proper definition to Christianity.

* * *

Whatever Christ's irony turns out precisely to be, it is certain that it is badly needed on the contemporary scene. For our own ironic images are in a state of pitiful disrepair. Our ironies are worn out, overflooding us, miserable in their lack of imagination, and we have grown flat and complacent in the use of them. It is the kind of moment when mediocre talents take over and when mediocre images, filled with the easy ironies of contempt, lacking in any charity or in the capacity to cause educating recognition, divide the culture groups. We are an overwhelmingly ironic generation. But irony, where it is separated from love, wisdom, and its own incomparable history, is the most miserable of all weapons or languages. At the moment, we are not very good at it. And I mean that phrasing ironically because it is a very mild way of describing a very serious situation.

2: Reimagining Faith

OF MY TWO SENSES OF IMAGES OF FAITH I TURN IMMEDIATELY
to my first sense and first question: What are my Images
of Faith? How do I imagine faith?

My first way of imagining faith in this chapter will be
to construct an image of it as a great primal and primitive force that precedes or even constructs knowledge
itself. Some of my metaphors for it as a very primal and
imaginable thing will be drawn from the powerful Greek
stories of Medea, the Furies, the House of Atreus, but
above all from the ecstatic but unironic figure of Dionysus—who will recur throughout this book as a master
image of primitive faith, ancient or modern. But under
this first and primal image we will also watch faith grow
into so mighty a torrent that it becomes the primal and
originating force in (1) human politics, (2) relationship,
and (3) thought. I will be proposing that it is not at all
external to these things, but deeply *internal,* in a way
that was not missed by Freud but has been misunder-
stood both by Kierkegaard and the modern pure objectivists.

My second way of imagining faith in the chapter will
fall under the all-important image and rubric of embodiment. If we want to see faith as imaginable we must
come to see how and in how many forms it is embodied,
has a horizontal as well as a vertical life. But I take the
liberty of avoiding confusion by forewarning that I will

be using this image of faith as embodied in various analogous ways. I will first imagine faith as abandoning its early childhood omnipotence and moving into the body of the finite world, into the articulated body of human knowledge; faith moves into the body of the sensibility of faith, a kind of home and atmosphere created by history and the Spirit; but most imaginably and visually of all it will march through an embodiment in the structure and politics of human society itself, where a whole nation like ours can receive grievous wounds if that embodiment is not being sustained within the necessary levels of social affection and belief in each other.

These are two principal ways in which I imagine faith. When this chapter is finished I will ask faith, so imagined in itself, to begin imagining the world, especially with those great ironic images of which Dionysus seems incapable.

A Primal Image of Faith

Let us hypothesize that faith is a first and primitive force in life; it is there, in a completely central and powerful way, from the beginning; it is not a sophisticated addition to knowledge, but a giant, universally operative force that is seeking proper objects, definitions, form, shape, people; rationality will later come in to help it in this search; people move onto its stage, to stay or go, succeed or fail (or, more usually, half succeed and half fail) to become objects and forms of faith. Irony tries to guide faith. Last of all, "in these days" Christ comes upon the pre-existing stage of faith, to

preempt it, to define and shape it, to declare that he is
the way, the truth, and the life.

*   *   *

The other and certainly more favorite sequence that
has guided our thoughts and feelings is the sequence
knowledge-faith. This, I think, has been one of our most
frequent modern images of faith, that it follows upon
knowledge, improves upon knowledge, is such a contribution to our picture of the world as human knowledge
could not have reached. This is an image with attendant
questions that it is well to deal with. But when it
becomes exclusive and preoccupying it creates a poor
methodology, for methodologies are created by the
questions we ask. And this central image seems to me to
create all kinds of subordinate images that have tended
to disturb the modern religious spirit. Today the advance of human knowledge has been truly astonishing.
How much can faith add to so vast a picture; does it not
rather seem to belong to a fringe-land of piety and
evangelism? What can faith add to the mighty mech-
anisms of evolution about which we know so much?
What can faith, coming along in the rear, be seen to add
to our knowledge of man through the modern mental
sciences? What does Christ add to Heidegger? Do not
these questions spawn an image of faith as a small thing
in a small corner? Let us try reversing our images. Let us
imagine, as I believe is indeed the case, that faith is a
mighty and primal force, to which even knowledge
contributes.

*   *   *

Immediate experience tells us that faith and unfaith are carved into the heart of man.

Even if we were to limit our speculations to the arena of the human heart we would not be able to escape the depth and the giant dimensions of the feelings involved in faith and unfaith. One way of imagining faith is to imagine its opposite. I cannot think of a more powerful example of the imagining of infidelity than the raging imagination of Medea, the Colchian princess, against Jason, the great Argonaut. She has been "terrible" in her fidelity to him. (Euripides' total description of her is that simple.) Through her magic Jason had overcome the bulls and dragons of Colchis to win the Golden Fleece and with it Medea herself. She caused her own brother Absyrtus to be slain for the sake of Jason. And for the sake of Jason she moved the daughters of Pelias to slay their father. In fidelity she follows him everywhere and gives up everything. But then, as though in a flash, Jason is to abandon her and his children for Creusa, the local princess of Corinth. We know the consequences, in rage and terror, as Medea strikes back. We can say that all that follows—Creusa in the fiery toils of the poisoned dress, Medea's children slaughtered by Medea, Jason wailing his new destiny at the hands of this barbarian woman—is the story of the imagining of unfaith by Medea. This is the way it looks to her. When we imagine something we are telling ourselves how it looks to us. Here we see faith in the image of its negative.

*   *   *

I repeat, then, that the instinct of faith is a torrent, powerful and primary. Medea is a good example of the power of the torrent for good and evil. When her faith collapses, when it realizes it has made a terrible mistake and "trusted the words of a Greek" the vacuum created by faith's disappearance is taken over by limitless fury. This fury is simply faith transformed into one of its dark forms. Now reasons, argument, language, rationality intervene to try to give shape to this dark form, but they fail.

> I know indeed what evil I intend to do,
> But stronger than all my after-thoughts is my fury,
> Fury that brings upon mortals the greatest evils.[1]

The Fury in this play of Euripides is an inward fury, a terrible human passion. In the earlier drama of Aeschylus the Furies are given a great cosmic form, but the idea and reality remains the same: the Furies insert themselves in a terrible way into human affairs precisely where the greatest faith has been violated, where a mighty word has been given but is now betrayed. In every case the Fury attacks the violator of a *word* written out in the most primitive and earthly forms of nature, the form of mother, who is word to her child, the form of wife, the form of friend, the form of father. All these forms are words carved out in the deepest realities of nature itself, making promises without opening the lips and demanding belief for very survival's sake. All the murders in the House of Atreus unleash the Furies because these murders strike against the most primal forms of faith. The energy and power of human faith become visible in the size of this fury. We tend to reduce faith to a sweet pious dimension, weak rival and challenger of knowledge. We know it better than that through its embodiment in fury. And through its encarvement, without words, in the very deepest structures of human life. Aristotle knew this well in *The Poetics* when he chose these violations of kinship and fidelity as the most tragic forms of tragedy. They are.

*　　*　　*

This is the advice Aristotle gives to the Greek poets who want to write plays in a truly tragic vein:

> Actions capable of this [tragic] effect must happen to persons who are either friends or enemies or indifferent to one another. If an enemy kills an enemy, there is nothing to excite pity—except so far as the suffering in itself is pitiful. So again with indifferent persons. But when the tragic incident occurs between those who are near or dear to one another—if, for example, a brother kills or intends to kill a brother, a son his father, a mother her son, a son his mother, or any other deed of the kind is done—these are the situations to be looked for by the poet.[2]

Here, too, we have the clue to the special horror of civil war or to those situations in which one social class, whether by violence or by images, rises against another in the same nation, in an excess that passes the point of the possibility of fundamental political life and the final bonds of social affection.

*　　*　　*

This faith, therefore, must be imagined as an enormous primitive force in man that is not yet educated, that hardly yet has a body, that as yet has only initial relation to the body of the world. It is beautiful, ecstatic, as yet unironic; it is mad and visionary; of all this the Greek god Dionysus was (and suddenly is again) the perfect representative. For those who are especially interested in this beautiful god—and who today in a for or against is not?—I recommend the reading of absorbing chapters on the Dionysiac cult in the fifth volume of Lewis Richard Farnell's *The Cults of the Greek States.* Then there is the very important *The Greeks and the Irrational* by E. R. Dodds, and, over the years, the divided commentaries on the *Bacchae* of Euripides by Dodds, Sandys, Murray, Norwood, Verrall, Winnington-Ingram, and others.[3] I say "divided" because these commentaries can no more agree on what to think of the god Dionysus, who is the central figure of the *Bacchae,* than we can. Nor can they agree about the meanings and decisions of Euripides himself.

So the question goes round and round, from then till now: What think we of Dionysus? The one thing that is certain is that we do think about the matter. And the opening sentences of Farnell are altogether indicative: "The study of the Dionysiac cult is one of the most attractive in the whole investigation into the religion of Hellas. . . . here, if anywhere, in the Greek peoples' worship, we may find traces of that fervour and self-abandonment which in our religious vocabulary is called faith." And a few pages later "the only quality [Homer] attaches to Dionysus is 'madness', the religious ecstasy with which the votary was inspired."[4]

Part of the meaning of Pentheus, king of Thebes, in

the *Bacchae* is that he is denying half of his humanity by denying and attacking Dionysus. This is no way to deal with Dionysus.

*   *   *

Dionysus is a god who is to be met upon the mountains, in the wild places. The Maenads, his followers, seek him upon the mountains, on Parnassos or in the vast ranges of Delphi, in wild and lonely ritual. He and they wish always to break out of the limits of any embodiment, for the sake of pure experience. He is the god not merely of wine but of the flower and the tree and every coursing, growing vein and thing in the earth. He is the god of life and of ecstasy, of the bull and the goat and the phallos, of all fruitfulness and productive vigor. He invades Greece from Thrace and Asia. He draws his worshipers to the mountains, in enthusiasm. The most native mental effect of the cult is a transcending of the limits of ordinary consciousness and the feeling of communion with the divine nature. In the great quarrel between him and Pentheus in the *Bacchae* he represents the explosion of sheer life against King Pentheus, the establishment. What do he and his followers experience?

The eternally beautiful odes of this great play give us some answer to this question. And Agave, in ecstasy, does go beyond consciousness. Her return to the body of this world is one of the most grievous roads the human spirit has ever traversed to come to a point of tragic recognition of the ambiguity of Dionysus. In mountain ecstasy she has torn her son Pentheus apart, limb from limb, head from shoulders, and is now bear-

ing the head home in disembodied triumph, so close is
the union of faith with hate before it moves into a fuller
life of the imagination. This will be faith and this the
way we must imagine it at its birth, before it grows a
body.

It is a beautiful and a terrible world, capable of all
things good and bad. How shall we accept it? But how
shall we reject it without drawing down on ourselves the
thunderbolts of Nietzsche, who in *The Birth of Tragedy*
blamed the ills of our new world on the conquest of
Dionysus by the rationality and the irony of Socrates.
Dionysus cannot be met by any irony but only by an
irony with more body but *as much passion.*

*   *   *

... the "enthusiast" is ἔνθεος, "full of the god",
the Maenad takes to herself the very name of the
god. Also the "enthusiast" possesses for the time
the power and the character of his deity, as Plato
tells us in the *Phaedrus;* the Maenads bring milk
and honey from river and rock, the daughters of
Anios can turn everything they touch into wine.
And there is method in the madness; for the wild
movements of the Bacchai, the whirling dance and
the tossing of the head, the frantic clamour and
music of the wind-instruments and tambourine, the
waving of the torches in the darkness, the drinking
of certain narcotics or stimulants, are recognized
hypnotic methods for producing mental seizure or
trance, and the drinking of the blood and eating
the raw-flesh of an animal that incarnated the god
is also a known form of divine communion.

And what are we to say of the "silence of the

Bakche," alluded to in the strangest of Greek proverbs? Is it the exhaustion that follows upon over-exaltation, or is it the very zenith reached by the flight of the spirit, when voices and sounds are hushed, and in the rapt silence the soul feels closest to God? [Farnell 5:161-162]

But the trouble is that Dionysus does not in reality confine his ecstasies to the mountains and to the places of solitude. Again and again he inhabits the political order, which he invades (and often creates) with ecstatic or mad forms of faith. In the actual play he invades the Greek city of Thebes (as many Dionysian faiths have invaded other actual worlds). But first the city had sinned by rejecting him and denying his divinity. Was it not part of the meaning of Euripides, therefore, that the political order was denying that any vision lay outside of itself?

But we know, better than any other period in history, what happens when the political order does indeed insist that there is vision in the world but that in the totality of its beliefs this vision must be contained in and fulfilled by the political order.

*   *   *

We have no stronger example of the modern emergence of Dionysus in the political order than the emergence of the mystique of total ecstasy, force, and the cult of the absolutely purified blood strain in the Führer's *Mein Kampf* and his creation of the National Socialist German Workers Party. There is good reason to believe that the seeds of both were being laid as early as 1909 in the agitated mind of this most unexpected form of Dionysus. But one must be restrained in pointing to the vast abysses of German intellectual history in the eighteenth and nineteenth centuries that this apocalypse might have drawn upon.

The clue to understanding the spirit of Dionysus is the brilliance and magnificence of its love and its hate, its capacity for both enthusiasm and destruction, together with its total ambiguity, its inability to keep these two forces together. It is always one or the other. He who neglects Dionysus entirely will share some small part of the fate of Pentheus in the *Bacchae* of Euripides! But that does not mean we may conspire with the profound evil in the other half of the heart of this god.

*   *   *

Dionysus is one of the most brilliant metaphors the human imagination has forged to describe that universal and primal force of faith which is so much larger a part of man than we have reckoned with. The trouble with Dionysus and his companion metaphors and myths is that if you stay with him too long, so fascinating is he in his haunts upon the mountain peaks, you are in danger of turning faith back into an exotic and finally inconsequential thing. Whereas it is a mighty and originating torrent that gets into the guts and interstices of most if not all of human politics, relationship, and thought.

*   *   *

Politics. I have only briefly suggested how primal faith creates or destroys the political order or drives it mad. In America it sometimes takes the form of power-

ful evangelical, perfectionistic (and masochistic) instincts that cannot possibly find full satisfaction in the
political order; but when they invade the political order
every six months, as they regularly do, they transform it
into a place of sheer excitement characterized by waves
of escalating fantasy. A national election campaign is a
wonder for the world to behold. Again primal faith and
unfaith is always ready to pounce with all its overcon-
centrated passion upon some event, or ready even to
create some pseudo-event to satisfy that passion. The
mark of what I am talking about is that the passion
always goes beyond the event and its reality—whether it
be the passion of the right over the advances of Com-
munism or of the left over Vietnam, Laos, Cambodia,
Kent State, Watergate. When the passion goes far beyond the certainty involved and far beyond the event it
can be called hysteria. And it tends repeatedly to drive
the national imagination toward a pinpoint. Because of
its absolute importance to society it is doubly necessary
to indicate when the intelligence itself is acting under
these pressures and in this way. Let me recall how
Richard Hofstadter warned this intelligence in his *Anti-
intellectualism in American Life:*

> He [the intellectual] may live for ideas, as I have
> said, but something must prevent him from living
> for *one idea,* from becoming obsessive or gro-
> tesque. Although there have been zealots whom we
> may still regard as intellectuals, zealotry is a defect
> of the breed and not of the essence. When one's
> concern for ideas, no matter how dedicated and
> sincere, reduces them to the service of some central
> limited preconception or some wholly external
> end, intellect gets swallowed by fanaticism. If there

is anything more dangerous to the life of the mind than having no independent commitment to ideas, it is having an excess of commitment to some special and constricting idea. The effect is as observable in politics as in theology: the intellectual function can be overwhelmed by an excess of piety expended within too contracted a frame of reference.[5]

Hofstadter tells us (pp. 134 ff.) that historically it has been the right and more deeply conservative end of the American political spectrum that has always inserted the theological passions of fundamentalist faith into politics; but now I think that it is the intelligence, and the academic intelligence, that is following suit. In such circumstances the intelligence does not emerge as one of the educators of primal faith; rather it conspires with the negative stages of primal faith. Above all it conspires in the production of exaggerated images, according to whose terms "Ordinary politics are the kingdom of darkness, ideological politics are the struggle of light against darkness."

This last citation is taken from a new book which is a treasure house for analysis of some of the questions raised in my present section: *The Intellectual and the Powers and Other Essays,* by Edward Shils.[6] Each reader must read this solid book for himself; my own way of reading it is to see the following as one of its major contributions: there is a vast difference between the superb competence of our academic culture in the area of its specializations and the mediocrity of its role as world of political opinion and political culture. It would be a temptation to argue from this dichotomy between superb competence and mediocrity that this is as things should be, that an intelligent physicist should not be expected to possess political intelligence. But I for one hesitate to accept this argument; it might finally lead us to conclude that the whole academic life of a nation can make no distinctive contribution to its politics, a position which, rightly, the intelligence can never accept. It is in fact very dubious that a nation can prosper if the academic community refuses its support; but it is even worse off if that community gives its support to an inward conformity and hysteria, a primal faith of its own. That, like primal faith itself, can be corrected.

*   *   *

Relationship. Despite my having just concluded that the political order regularly erupts into attempts to find complete satisfaction in politics itself for primal faith, it is no solution to say that faith must be kept out of the order of politics. Rather, I will soon be saying that faith creates political society. Now, as our even wider point, we can only hint at or guess at the manner in which it makes itself the very cement of all human relationship, so strong is it as an originating and building force. In any human situation where the alternatives are the choice between an individualistic or narcissistic construction of the facts on the one hand and a human and social construction on the other, it is finally faith alone that permits us to make the decisive move from a narcissistic, self-enclosed world to a public world. But it is only at the point of this decision that the whole order of true human feelings and truly human sensibility becomes possible. The purely private is always ugly; there is no beauty in it.

Let me cite a crucial passage from Freud which I have

used in another place, it is so good, and which brings together the orders of faith, relationship, and the world:

When the patient has to fight out the normal conflict with the resistances which we have discovered in him by analysis, he requires a powerful propelling force to influence him toward the decision we aim at, leading to recovery. Otherwise it might happen that he would decide for a repetition of the previous outcome, and allow that which had been raised into consciousness to slip back again under repression. The outcome in this struggle is not decided by his intellectual insight—it is neither strong enough nor free enough to accomplish such a thing—but solely by his relationship to the physician. In so far as his transference bears the positive sign, it clothes the physician with authority, transforms itself into faith in his findings and in his views. Without this kind of transference or with a negative one, the physician and his arguments would never even be listened to. Faith repeats the history of its own origin; it is a derivative of love and at first it needed no arguments. Not until later does it admit them so far as to take them into critical consideration if they have been offered by someone who is loved. Without this support arguments have no weight with the patient, never do have any with most people in life. A human being is therefore on the whole only accessible to influence, even on the intellectual side, in so far as he is capable of investing objects with libido; and we have good reason to recognize, and to fear, in the measure of his narcissism a barrier to his susceptibility to influence, even by the best analytic technique.[7]

*   *   *

Knowledge. We are already halfway into our next step, the step in which we reflect on powerful and primal faith as internal fashioner and constructor of endless forms of knowledge itself. It is so far from being external or irrelevant to knowledge that it is often the very internal shaper of knowledge. This vision of the powerful internality of faith will only be understood if we see in a moment how two of the most influential modern visions of faith have been visions of faith as incredibly external to our seeing of things and people.

Over against these two external images, I am about to say that faith and unfaith become the very interstices of manifold shapes of knowledge, a very atmosphere that determines the structures of things and people in our world. Another way of putting the matter, apparently very intricate but in reality the simple substance of everyday thought, is that as there is no such thing as a purely given fact or image, neither is there such a thing as purely objective and external evidence for, say, someone's friendship or someone's goodness or for the presence and activity of God in our lives; faith, as driving, creative force, is internally present to these images, giving them their shape.

*　　*　　*

If I approach a man with the paradigms of faith, I compose his actions accordingly. The patterns and interpretation shifts completely if I approach him without faith (as perhaps I should, for that matter). I compose the "evidence" in another way. But this is a two-way street. For not only does each one of us approach the world with or without faith; it is also necessary that each one of us *be approached* with faith; we have to be believed in by somebody, by man and/or by God. This is what Martin Buber calls *being confirmed*.

Not only faith is a gift. So is it a gift *to be believed-in.* We are created and patterned by the faith of others. It, too, is an air to breathe in. If this need is not recognized, if it is not reasonably handled and actuated, it will run out of control and amuck; it can go mad with need.

*   *   *

1. The externality of Kierkegaard. Just as it is doubtful that there is any such thing as observation of a pure fact or a pure image, it is also questionable whether there be such a thing as pure evidence. A common definition of faith is: that which is built out of something more than evidence and does not act on "pure evidence." And so it is the evidence of things not seen, the substance of things hoped for. Faith does not see; it hears from another. But then the temptation is to think of faith as that which leaps beyond the evidence. I have never been happy with this image of faith, and I consider it to be a romantic oversimplification of a much more complicated, but also more ordinary, human mode of action. First of all, it is a romantic image. It is at the heart of Kierkegaard's image of faith and of the Great Knight of Faith—who will not be ruled by the depersonalizing domination of any objective system, who will finally only find that greatest objectivity which is God through that most intense subjectivity which is a faith of the leap, of the risk, of that commitment which, even if it is wrong, will lead into rightness by force of its own sincerity and authenticity. This is romantic. It acts

x But note, this is done in the name of passion.

without evidence, or against the evidence or outside the evidence. It is without true strength, for it does not shape the reality of people and things.

The sequence on faith may be described in the following way. It does not see; then it hears (the word of God or man); then it inserts this paradigm of hearing into its seeing, its imagining, its experiencing the world.

*   *   *

2. The new externality. It is ironic that at this later date the idea of authenticity and sincerity has now swung full cycle into the opposite of Kierkegaard's understanding of the matter. I think that the latter-day interpreters are wrong too, but the fact is that the situation has swung full circle. Now you are declared inauthentic, insincere, craven, if you leap one step beyond the evidence and are faithless to it. We see no virtue at all in a leap of faith, nor any strength in it. The only faith now respected is one that follows a complete objectivity of knowledge.

But surely the more important thing is that the human mind simply does not work in either of these two ways when the question is one of faith, even if it be the highest religious faith. In his corner of speculation Kierkegaard was demanding an absolute subjectivity of his Knight of Faith, a subjectivity that would escape determination by the outside and finite world of evidence. Now in this later world the new demand of the new sincerity is for an absolute objectivity which will be completely faithful to evidence, even if it is the evidence for absurdity. I think that both views are wrong. Why?

*   *   *

In both cases there is a mechanical view of evidence. In the first case (Kierkegaard) the evidence is purely external to faith and "objective," and *must be overcome by faith* precisely because it is external and objective. In the second case the evidence is completely "objective" and *must be adhered to by faith* precisely because and after it is objective. In each case, the action of faith, though entirely different, is a definition of sincerity and authenticity. But for me the important thing is that in the two cases the image of faith and its moment of decision is an image of something external to the evidence. The evidence remains pure—that is to say, it remains untouched by faith. In neither case, neither with Kierkegaard nor the complete objectivists, is there an understanding that there must indeed be evidence but that *it is found, collected and composed by faith itself.* Faith, like the imagination, is a constantly active, shaping, re-shaping and creative principle. Furthermore, if this is the case, it is also a suffering principle, always passing through a suffering phase until it succeeds in shaping or reshaping the evidence. It is always historical and its task is never done. My meaning in making these points may not yet be clear, but I do not intend to abandon the point without later elaboration. Meanwhile, I have only wished to give a first sketch of faith as energizer and shaping originator of politics, relationship, and knowledge.

An Embodied or Horizontal Image of Faith

In my *second* image of faith I am presenting it as enjoying a truly embodied and horizontal life. It would be foolhardy to summarize the life of the imagination or the whole of an aesthetic under any single rubric. The notion of the finding or creating of embodiment for a thing or an idea or a person or a society, if it is to be imagined and literally become seen, is single but it is not narrow. It comes close to the heart of large as well as small ventures of the human imagination. That the creation of embodiment is the best source and possibility for the best knowledge of things is the key to the understanding of the revolutionary work of Giambattista Vico (1688–1744) in his vigorous attack on Cartesian principles of clear and distinct ideas and self-consciousness as the better fonts of vision. The essence of his own theory of knowledge was first contained in his *De antiquissima Italorum sapientia,* but the *Scienza Nuova,* despite the frequent presence of exaggerated and exaggerating materials, is the monumental contribution of Vico to European civilization. The inventive principle behind all his work is the identity between the *verum* (the truth of things) and the *factum* (that which is made or created by man himself).

We know best what we make ourselves, history, law, language, society, myth. These mighty things are man creating himself and making himself visible to himself. In my language—and I take the liberty of pushing Vico into my present language—these mighty things give body and embodiment to man and are man imagined by himself, in terms not of clear ideas but of the body of a world. Man is a creature who can only be understood historically, in the terms and the light of and the body of his own history.

(I wish to note now that my own later elucidation of the nature of faith will depend on the image of faith not only as embodied but also as "historical," as something, that is, that can be best understood as we watch it move through the stages of the life of man and the life of Christ. This is the way that faith has always been best imagined, but we are not sufficiently conscious that this has been the case).

*   *   *

But the best, the clearest, and perhaps the most classical example of imagining or experiencing something through a masterly act of embodiment was already and continues to be *The Republic* of Plato. It is at its heart and center an act of embodiment; this is its whole methodology. It has raised a question which can be answered satisfactorily in no other way. The question is: is human goodness (or "justice" or "righteousness"— δικαιοσύνη) worthwhile? Is it worthwhile in itself; that is to say, let us no longer ask about it in terms of externality, in terms of its profits, the reputation, the friends, the business it brings; let us even conceive that the consequences are the very opposite, and that, without friends or reputation, we land on a cross for our goodness? Is the thing in itself, naked, bereft, worthwhile?

If we attempt some extremely limited vision of this thing through purely individual and introspective methods, we will get nowhere. If only we could find this inward thing carved out in larger form, in letters that would be carved in monumental form on the side of a mountain, then the question might be answerable. But there is such a great form or body; it is the state (we would now say human society) which is the larger body of man. . . .

I will not continue my own analysis, but if one reads backward and forward from the key numbers 368 and 369 in the second of the ten books of *The Republic,* one will be able with a sure touch to watch the building of the body and this extraordinary back and forth between the soul or the center of man on the one hand and this larger body on the other. Though it was easier for the Greeks; they had not made our dichotomies between ethics and politics.

What is the final argument of *The Republic?* It is simply this. He who truly imagines goodness, he who successfully imagines it, needs no other argument.

It is in these directions of embodiment, and of social embodiment at that, that I would like my own thoughts on the imagining and experiencing of faith to move. But I am not a sociologist or a political scientist. When I am imagining the body of faith I shall also be imagining its center and vertical life.

*   *   *

Can faith be thus embodied and thus imagined? I think it can. It can be experienced and imagined if we conceive that it has not only a vertical life, directed in the most formal way toward God, but a horizontal life as well, directed toward creating and being the very essence of the life of man in society and politics. If this is so, then faith not only has a center and a soul but a body as well. And so hard and deep is the relationship of faith to society that it is wrong for religious men to say that they apply or "relate" the principles of faith to society (make them relevant!). All such external language misses the point and, despite all straining and good will, is condemned to the agonizing irrelevance it strives so much to avoid. Human society is faith itself. And I do not mean thereby that religious belief, that is to say belief in God, makes society. *To say, rather, that belief in God has a body, and that that body is the belief men have in each other, and that this constitutes human society comes much closer to what I mean.* And it leaves faith less external to life. When faith descends to being relevant it traps itself in another pitiful situation.

*   *   *

Does faith have a body?

It was the intervention of Scripture itself and common sense that told us how ghostly a thing love would be without a body, and how false. In the case of love, theology has been very active on the vertical and the horizontal level, on the level of God and man, on the level of idea and body. We have no doubt that we cannot love God unless we love man.

But the lack of an embodying act of the imagination had already occurred in the case of hope. If ever there was a situation, we thought, where we should fall back on God alone, without the intervention of a horizontal level, it was that of hope. We had told ourselves that the whole horizontal level of the world could not be hoped in and would some day fade away. What else is there to hope in but God? But there was the critical fact that the building and survival of the city of man and of human civilization deeply involves our hope in each other and our depending on each other. It is certainly necessary to know how and whom to mistrust. But if we are to hope in God alone, if hope is not to have a body on the

] 57 [

horizontal level, then heaven is and will be occupied by the cynics and by those who have no real power of hope. How stand our questions in the case of faith?

*   *   *

One can hardly think of a purer version of verticality and pure encounter theory than the following by Romano Guardini in an otherwise beautiful book, *The Life of Faith*. (Such a version avoids all the life of the body, the total possibility of faith. Faith finally has no body. This is a vision that I must reject completely).

> According to its manifestations, acts or attitudes, faith flows in structures according to the predispositions of different individuals; but the call of God affects one elsewhere, and the decision to be made lies elsewhere. We may perhaps distinguish between the "body" and "soul" of faith. The body of faith differs according to various dispositions, countries, ages and human circumstances; but its soul—or more exactly the seat of its soul—is everywhere independent of determinations. At this depth—as we have already noticed—there is only pure encounter between the human identity and God. Through all the variations of structure and aptitude, this supreme encounter is the essential thing.[8]

If this is true, then faith really has no true body, according to my sense of that word.

*   *   *

When I use the phrase "the body of faith," I use it analogously. That is to say, it has a number of related

] 58 [

meanings, principal among which is the human community. But all the meanings will deal with the concrete,
horizontal, and imaginable part of the life of faith.

It is impossible to decide that we will deal with faith
in some untouched way on the vertical level and will
transcend the victories and failures of the body of our
faith. Yet this has been one of our basic images of the
theological virtues. We have proposed that faith can be
isolated at a pure center.

It does not make sense to assume the possibility of a
"pure metaphysics" or a pure faith which can transcend
our present state of affairs, can ignore our present
images and feelings about reality, and pass on and up to
a serene reflection on pure existence (as though we can
be one thing in one world and another thing in another
world). It is surely better to come to that exalted point
by passing through where we now are—because "where
we now are" is the substance of ourselves.

*   *   *

First of all, let me use the word "body" somewhat
literally. Let it mean my actual self. There must be a
constant dialogue between faith and *this* body; there
cannot be this sharp distinction between the soul and
the body of faith.

The fundamental image of faith must be dramatic and
corporeal: that is to say, we must *move through* the self,
through its history and sensibility, not away from it. Or
if we move away from it, it can only be by moving
through it. Any other way involves despair or impossibility. It is only and precisely *I* who believe that *I* am
the subject of redemption and resurrection. Surely it is

the half of realistic belief that it is precisely this more miserable embodied self that will be redeemed.

*   *   *

The embodying action of faith (and the imagination) has the most elemental beginnings. The first is the struggle to reach into existence itself.

An important point to start from in any serious attempt to explore the role of imagination in theology (or in life for that matter) is the relationship of faith and the imagination to existence. Let us suppose that it is the imagination which finds or makes what we call "reality," that visual-conceptual image of our finite, our objective, our existent world. In saying that, we are at the center of the life of the imagination and of the physiology of faith. Then we must realize that finding or making existence is a difficult task. How to fit all things together in some way that is even *partly* understandable? It involves a struggle and a wrestling, like Jacob wrestling with the angel. We cannot decide: I will struggle with God and not with the earth. That is really no decision at all, or at best a decision not to wrestle. But where we do make the decision to deal with existence, then epistemology and faith can best meet at the initial point of finite reality itself. I hypothesize that without faith the mind cannot enter into existence at all, even at the most elementary point.

We have reason now to know that the mind leaves what seems paradise when it first engages in real thought with the world, much less with God. The new sciences of the mind tell us we leave omnipotence. The specific thought whereby, leaving *this* paradise, the mind wrestles with anything less than omnipotence has faith carved into the very guts of this act by which it lays hold of the precise density of any actual thing. The very weight and shape and form not only *take* faith to lay hold of, but it *is* a faith. It gives up the feeling of omnipotence to acknowledge the existence of this other limited thing. It is the beginning of the body of faith. We are first coaxed into it, as infants, by those who love us. We enter, in thought and action, because we trust them.

Faith, therefore, is required to move into the step after step processes of rational knowledge. And all rational and scientific knowledge follows faith in sequence.

*   *   *

Let me take an added look at the chasm that exists between the omnipotence of the child that feels like power and those first and then continued steps into the world of definite objects and limited forms that lead into the whole articulated world, the world of the adult, the world of thought, science, and the arts.

But let us see first that if there is a chasm between the two, it is a necessary chasm. The first form of faith the child immediately develops is a faith in this his omnipotence: his wishes are identical with reality; he thinks he has but to wish in order to achieve every possible gratification of instinctual need. Without this first faith, illusory though it be, the child could not survive. (The same may be truer than we think of the Dionysian stage of faith, in history and the individual.) It is a brilliant, enthusiastic, and ecstatic state, completely ambiguous, shifting with ease from love to hate in the presence of deprivation and the unexpected; but, for all that, it is a stage whose shoals we must pass through with the growing help of irony (and the final irony of Christ). The victory of irony, we shall see, will be that it will manage to keep the experiences of love and hate together and will not separate them into two absolute experiences of ecstatic love and ecstatic destruction.

With the passage into the articulated world of objects and of time the child accomplishes a great journey, a journey which requires a new faith, this time a faith in the precise forms of objects and the steps of time. But psychoanalytic studies of childhood tell us that it is the child's faith in a mother figure who knows how to mix deprivation with gratification that weans it from omnipotence to the world of separated and separate objects.

I call special attention to the fact that this is the first and basic and continuing confrontation of the human spirit with the relationship between the smaller and the larger lines of life and the world that I have chosen as one of the most central images of this book. We have met the first victory of the smaller line, in this case a victory of objects and knowledge over omnipotence. It is a victory that is preceded and guided by faith.

*   *   *

We must only suppose, recalling our childhood—but can be reasonably sure of it—that reality comes as a shock when we first enter it, and it is a shock that it is heavy, has corners and edges, shines, glows, burns, tastes, and can ache and give great pain. Above all, it is resistant, you cannot go through it, it will not go away. A good deal of our thinking about God wants to make these qualities of really being there go away; at least he is not that way! We say we abstract from limitation and call it God. We have often abstracted from the actual existence of things and called it God. So we say that God is not heavy like iron. But suppose I say that he is even more actual than iron, meaning that if you think the iron is really there, that is the direction to take to imagine that God is there. But as the mind often does now, in its search for God, there is only a ghost at the end of the process, and very little existence or faith. We should reverse this process and keep the stress on the existence of things. This is where the imagination comes in. *The task of the imagination is to imagine the real.* At the end of tragedy man comes in contact with existence, with the real thing. What I call the realistic imagination always does.

We must think in the same way about faith. We are accustomed to ask: what has this fey, transcendental, religious thing to do with the hustle and bustle, the burn and the iron of life? But it is there, as large and as hard as the everyday life of nations and human society.

*   *   *

In faith there is a need of a unique combination of sentiments and ideas, faith and questioning, seriousness and irony, illusion and reality. I call it "the body of the sensibility of faith." It has taken several thousands of years to shape this sensibility for what it is, a complex, a highly developed instrument for the handling of many things, birth, life, death, and faith itself. Faith, therefore, is not an isolated thing, limited to some secret place in the soul.

We know a good deal about literary sensibility. We know a good deal about the broad thing called human sensibility. But faith, too, is and has a developed sensibility with a good deal of work and history behind it. What about the Spirit? Surely this is the way the Spirit works. It does not merely work from a spiritual, a disembodied center that will survive all the ravages of history because it does not need a history. With us and in us it makes history. But history also makes the body of sensibility of faith. Part of the truth about original sin is that we are born into an atmosphere, a world, of hate and anxiety. But part of grace is that we are also born into a world of faith, a real atmosphere and general sensibility which is a historical construction of God and the Church. It is the Spirit of Christ, not an ideology but an actual historical spirit. It is a body of faith, making faith most imaginable. It is embodied in books, actions, histories, lives, deaths, in the endless areas of a thing called an atmosphere, and above all in the person of Christ, enlarged into such a body as Plato could not have expected.

*   *   *

Let us see if it helps to think of faith not only at an originating center (faith in the absolute word of God, without the support of evidence or intrinsic rationality) but at its periphery, in the world of a full, embodied life, where faith comes out as a highly developed construct of character, sensibility, judgments, images, reactions.

There is a real possibility that by any confinement of faith to the center we may be doing grave injustice to the center itself. Let me put the matter somewhat melodramatically. Would Karl Barth have held so long and so tenaciously to *his* dialectical understanding of the center and ultimate character of faith if he had allowed into his understanding of it the facts that he always started the day by listening to Mozart and that he made one of the great theological stands against Hitler? Karl Barth was a very great man who knew by adult instinct and without effort that the faith of his Lord and the lordship of Christ could not tolerate or accept certain forms of the political order and the ecstasies they try to engender. It is thus by indirection, but by profound indirection, that faith at its political periphery can show what it is at its center.

If we look at the periphery we may find what really is or should be at the center.

*   *   *

There is next, therefore, that body of faith which is human society.

The men of faith-as-pure-encounter theory tell us that there is a body of contingent and historical elements in faith, but that, finally, there is the soul of faith, the real thing.

But suppose faith has a body, in the city of man. Suppose it has a history and a communal "state of affairs." Is it not possible that the state of faith, in a group or nation, can be quite clear, for good and bad? Is it immaterial to faith that we are in the presence of vast waves of unfaith and distrust among men, cultural groups, social groups, nations?

We are in the habit of asking: What is the state of

religious faith in the United States? Can we broaden the question (without really changing it) and ask: What is the state of faith in the United States? How will this, especially this vast state of contempt and disbelief among us, affect religious faith?

*   *   *

The writing of these thoughts began at what was probably the hightide, in my country, of the crisis of the Vietnam War. For years we were surrounded by this thing as by the whole of reality. Yet there are those—I am one of them—who think it will soon prove an incident in the midst of larger, almost undetected, events. We can disagree about the nature of these larger events, but I give my own version of what really is happening, and will happen, as I write. I think that we are, nationally, in the middle of larger events by far. We are in the middle of a vast cultural crisis and division. The real war is at home. It takes the form not of the usual political divisions—savage and enjoyable as these can be—but of a complete collapse of faith between the two cultural groups that constitute the nation: the intellectuals and the middle class. We are not only in the presence of the failure of belief (there is no belief left, the one class in the other); the lack of belief is intensifed by a mutual contempt and fear such as has not often existed between two national groups in modern history. Our crisis over the Vietnam War was a trifle compared to this interior war and collapse of faith. I do not mean transcendental faith, but the body of faith.

Nor am I saying at all that the war of the cultures is a war between those who have religious faith and those who do not. For those who have transcendental faith are as wounded in the body of their faith as those who do not have it. Hilaire Belloc used to say that either a man believed or he did not, that there were no halves in believing. If what I am now saying is true, then his statement is false. For faith, if it has embodiment, can grow sick, recieve wounds, grow weak and almost die. There can be such a thing as states of faith. And these states are as visible and imaginable as states of physical disease in hospitals.

Can we experience faith and its absences? At times I wish we could not.

*　　*　　*

Now, unhappily, it is becoming easier to imagine faith, to form an image of it. Our problem vanishes for the imagination. Faith or the lack of it is in the veins of everything, constituting or destroying. It is the hard iron of everyday life. It is so present to us that it can bring us to the verge of a civil war of the emotions. No matter what side one is on, it is necessary to recognize that we are in the presence, when in the presence of faith, of a torrential power for good and evil, about which we can say: there is no difficulty in imagining *this.* Now it begins to be an understatement to state that faith has a body. This body is the actuality, or the death, of the human community.

*　　*　　*

If one of the principal tasks, if not the total task, of the imagination is to articulate the parts and jointings of that which it beholds, language, which is so endlessly generative of articulated sound and meaning structures, is surely one of the most constant and imposing embodiments of the human imagination. But we are increasingly agreed that there is no such thing as a private language; all language is public and a public act; in all my language I pledge that what I say is what I think; according to the code and game and life of language I make a pledge and expect belief—not belief in what I say, for we expect to find out that we are fools or stupid or mistaken, but belief that what I say is what I think. Language then belongs to the very marrow of the body of faith.

Faith is more than willing to accept fools into its body, and every imaginable stupidity—because this is all within the code or the language of faith—but a deliberate politization of language which declares that language need not be the imagining of the mind speaking but must serve political and class-culture purpose is, despite its sophistication, a diseased attack on the body of faith. The argument used to defend this attack on language is this: it is impossible to be neutral about the world; there is no such thing as a pure objectivity without a point of view. But there is a horrendous distance between this argument—which can be discussed—and its conclusion: that it is not only a good thing, it is nobility itself to distort the truth and language. The universities should be the final defenders of language. But the universities have often been declared politicized.

*   *   *

What happens to a civilization when language begins to lose its meaning or is no longer believed in, or when everything begins to mean its opposite, or when objectivity is mocked, or when language (and the press) is politicized, when, in brief, language loses its relationship to faith.

It was the collapse of mutual faith and of language that in great part led to the beginning of the collapse of civilization among the Greek city states at the close of the fifth century B.C. The following is a famous part of the embodied image of unfaith we are given by Thucydides after he has finished the specific story of the ordeal among the citizens of Corcyra.

So revolutions broke out in city after city, and in places where the revolutions occurred late the knowledge of what had happened previously in other places caused still new extravagances or revolutionary zeal, expressed by an elaboration in the methods of seizing power and by unheard-of atrocities in revenge. To fit in with the change of events, words, too, had to change their usual meanings. What used to be described as a thoughtless act of aggression was now regarded as the courage one would expect to find in a party member; to think of the future and wait was merely another way of saying one was a coward; any idea of moderation was just an attempt to disguise one's unmanly character; ability to understand a question from all sides meant that one was totally unfitted for action.

Fanatical enthusiasm was the mark of a real man, and to plot against an enemy behind his back was perfectly legitimate self-defense. Anyone who held violent opinions could always be trusted, and anyone who objected to them became a suspect.

To plot successfully was a sign of intelligence, but it was still cleverer to see that a plot was hatching. If one attempted to provide against having to do either, one was disrupting the unity of the party and acting out of fear of the opposition. In short, it was equally praiseworthy to get one's blow in first against someone who was going to do wrong, and to denounce someone who had no intention of doing any wrong at all. Family relations were a weaker tie than party membership, since party members were more ready to go to any extreme for any reason whatever. . . .

Revenge was more important than self-preservation. And if pacts of mutual security were made, they were entered into by the two parties only in order to meet some temporary difficulty, and remained in force only so long as there was no other weapon available. When the chance came, the one who first seized it boldly, catching his enemy off his guard, enjoyed a revenge that was all the sweeter from having been taken, not openly, but because of a breach of faith. It was safer that way, it was considered, and at the same time a victory won by treachery gave one a title for superior intelligence. And indeed most people are more ready to call villainy cleverness than simple-mindedness honesty. They are proud of the first quality and ashamed of the second.

Love of power, operating through greed and through personal ambition, was the cause of all these evils. . . .

. . . there was a general deterioration of character throughout the Greek world. The simple way of looking at things, which is so much the mark of a noble nature, was regarded as a ridiculous quality and soon ceased to exist. Society had become divided into two ideologically hostile camps, and each side viewed the other with suspicion. As for ending this state of affairs, no guarantee could be given that would be trusted, no oath sworn that people would fear to break; everyone had come to the conclusion that it was hopeless to expect a permanent settlement and so, instead of being able to feel confident in others, they devoted their energies to providing against being injured themselves.[9]

*   *   *

When the body of faith enters into a period of great crisis in a community the immediate visual faculties of human beings seem to enter into a remarkable state of near derangement. That solid if realistic belief in each other which I have been calling the body of faith is not a purely intellectual situation. It is accompanied by a whole life of powerful attitudes and feelings. Perhaps all these are least noticed, as powerfully present, when they are working well. But when the negative appears the reserve set of attitudes and feelings pour dramatically and melodramatically into the air. Above all this death of horizontal faith affects our very vision. I mean the literal thing we call vision: the seeing of things. Waves of fantasy pour into the atmosphere. The two culture classes see each other as monsters, no less. The consequences of the combination of linguistic and visual distortion are quite extraordinary. We can calculate that there must be an extraordinary negative life and set of drives here which require their own joy and satisfaction and which lead to a constant escalation in the images of a nation. When one joins this to another act of politicization—I would cite as evidence the politicizing of our cinematic images in the last five years—you are certain to have developed an extreme "state of the images" which begins to lose touch with reality.

* * *

If neither faith nor history nor anything else gets into the images, then I repeat that the imagination falls into a Cartesian situation. If this is true it is ironic, because the intention of Descartes and Cartesianism was to separate *thought* out from everything else but itself, from all imagining as well, and thus achieve a clear foundation for all thinking.

But now transfer this intention, ironically, to the imagination. Place the imagination at the topmost peak of the head, where it has lost touch with the body, with limitation, with ordinary human sensibility, with reasonable anticipations of a future, with some memory of the past, with faith and history. Then especially do all this where images are fantastically multiplied and literally "produced" for a whole people. The imagination then becomes, with a vengeance, not a separate faculty, but a separated *world,* with no obligations to yesterday or tomorrow. What becomes possible, and probable, are vast waves of fantasy or vast escalations of ordinary images.

Under these conditions the "state of the images" is not anything in which one can place faith.

* * *

Faith has its own images of the political order and it is precisely these images which are its great creative contribution to politics. It is because these images descend to such levels of the imagination that we can say: faith creates or makes possible the political order. It reaches a depth of political unity. It is only when the categories, the differences between us, announce themselves as final, and when the contempt of one category for another loses sight of these images made by faith that the political order is in danger of real collapse. We cannot play with images the way we are doing without paying a great price. It is a game. It is the most volatile of games. And the vilest. I do not mean politics. I mean playing with this point of depth of the imagination, playing with the exaltation of the categories, especially with the exaltation of the intelligence over those who have a lesser and less beautiful share of it. After twenty-six million years we are suddenly in a great hurry and we announce, grandiloquently and feverishly, without irony, the worst of times.

The imagination must grasp a point of depth beyond which, in any event, we cannot go or underneath which we cannot sink without the destruction of the most elementary faith and thus of human society. This point exists below all the categories (of rich and poor, the intelligence and the bourgeoisie, right and wrong, black and white, even good and evil). It is the dramatic space seized hold of for the acting out of their characters by Aeschylus in *The Seven Against Thebes* and by Sophocles in the *Antigone*.

The two principal actors of my point, alive throughout *The Seven* and dead throughout the *Antigone,* are Polyneices and Eteocles, the two sons of Oedipus who contend for the kingship in Thebes to the tragic point, though brothers, of the slaying of each other. Creon, the new ruler after the endless pity of such strife, declares for difference *at this point,* resurrects the categories, honors one body, Polyneices, as absolutely good and dishonors the other corpse, Eteocles, as absolutely evil. Antigone, eternal sister, takes her stand and declares against the categories at this level of death and the unbreakable brotherhood of final human destiny. She will not tolerate, nor will the Greek faith, that a dead brother be so dishonored.

Ironically, it is only if this point is seized and preserved by the imagination that we can afford to let the categories of life and the reason reemerge. Every manner of pluralism and dissent becomes possible and will themselves be generated by this point. No doubt I will shock by saying that even war will become possible, if it remains war between *human* beings.

It begins to be doubtful if, nationally, we are preserving our grip on this deep place of the imagination. The odds begin to be that it is being flooded and swept away by fantasy, the fantasy of the absolute black and white of the categories.

These categorical images of the political order are voluble, arrogant, and "magnificent" in the negative sense of that word. They are quarrelsome to an extreme and deal with faith's image of the political order by calling it compromise. They are simplistic and refuse debate. They are melodramatic examples of large lines overwhelming and smothering the smaller but deeper lines of faith. They have no irony in them by which they might question their own easy, short-term victories. But if it is irony that is lacking today in the body of our faith, let us now ask what that irony is. It makes less noise but is very mighty.

PART TWO

FAITH IMAGINING
THE WORLD

3: The Structure of the Irony of Faith

SO MUCH FOR THE SUBJECT OF THE IMAGES WE HAVE OF FAITH.
These have been some few of the ways in which we can
imagine faith. But thus far so much has been only
preface to the more important question: How does faith
experience the world?

There are only two alternatives in deciding what
method to follow here. One could speak very widely
about a good number of the ways according to which
faith composes the world and say a comparative little
about each, with all the dissatisfaction and immediate
superficiality such a decision compels. Or one could
develop some central way in which faith images reality,
one that is sufficiently flexible and wide ranging in the
materials it involves and the paths it takes, preferably
some heuristic image that leads to many insights other
than itself. This seems by far the better course. I therefore choose to explore the ironic images of faith, the
irony of faith, the irony of Christ. This may seem a
sophisticated and an academic rubric under which to
study faith, but my hope is that that simply is not so
and that things will turn out altogether differently.
Moreover, when I look for irony I look for the irony of
Christ; that irony is nothing apart from his life and his
passage through it.

I want to stress my own strong feelings against any

limitation of faith's imagination to some one image, no matter how good or powerful, and against any limitation of God-talk to some one way, no matter now effective or contemporary. Fortunately, in electing to study the irony of faith and its images, I have not only elected a single way of imagining—as a limitation of space and not of faith—but I have chosen one that can, happily, ironize or criticize or keep in place any single image that proposes itself as absolute.

How shall faith think vertically about God and horizontally about the world? In every possible way.

*　　*　　*

Faith is not bound to some single image or way of experiencing the world.

The mind and imagination is crippled by the gathering intensity of the single approach, the approach that finally reaches a pinpoint in its range of visions and flexibility. The method sticks to one area of imagination; it is as though by wearing down that area and only that area it bruises and wounds it, so that finally even this area is not able to do its work; it grows rigid and dark from the intensity. Moreover this kind of effort is based on the mistaken assumption that it is possible, by effort, by sincerity, by goodness, by passion, and by the absolute correctness of some single logic or image to make a kind of absolute breakthrough at some single point in this crucial question. And perhaps one of our assumptions here is that God, if he had so chosen, could certainly have given or could now give some single point of evidence or proof that would be beyond all cavil or doubt. But Christ himself seemed to reject this idea when he told his contemporaries that even if the dead rose from the dead to give witness they would not be believed.

*   *   *

I somewhat hesitate to speak here of the work of Ian T. Ramsey which so many of us so much admire. He has done a few eminent books and many articles which try to reconcile the new logical and linguistic philosophy with religious experience. He is inclined to talk of "models" of human experience which become cosmic disclosures of God, and to veer away from uses of a word like *image* because of its psychological and non-philosophical reverberations. Whereas I find myself searching for words (like *images* and *imaging the world*) that come nearer to the people's way of speaking. But these differences being said, I have a profound respect for all his instincts as a religious thinker. So in the present case of the intellectual's desperate search for *a* proper way of talking about God, suddenly the ordinary man finds that methodologically he is doing very well:

> Let me [recall] that at one time, and in the Old Testament in particular, people made free use of all kinds of pictures, images, metaphors, models in their talk about God. No one has illustrated this more plainly than Eric Heaton in his book *His Servants the Prophets* where he remarks that in the Old Testament, "Yahweh's" relationship to his people is represented under the figures of a father, mother, nurse, husband, friend, warrior, shepherd, farmer, metal-worker, builder, potter, fuller, physician, judge, tradesman, king, fisherman, and scribe—to mention, at random, only a few of the activities of the community.

] 79 [

All this does not mean that we are to remain steadfast to a given set of Old Testament images, are not to substitute our own more experienced language. And all these images or models must stay in modifying, organic competition with one another. Moreover, the life of each human being, like the life of Christ, is a new and separate image.

But Ramsey also has a sense of humor, and he knows that there is such a thing as balance and unbalance in the development of all our metaphors. He warns, as well he might, against the endless preoccupation with detail in the use of "theological models."

> Theological assertions are not flat or uniform as we might say "the cat is on the mat" is flat and uniform. If we speak of God catching men in his net, and gathering them in his drag, do not let us have such an interest in fishing that we revel in developing discourses of the net and the drag. . . . [1]

These are important words, with which I heartily sympathize, but because of the very subject and fundamental methodology of this book I have, inevitably, more difficulty with this point than Ramsey. For one thing I am intent on creating, and in a very imaginable way, a body for faith and, very specially, a political and social embodiment of faith. How much shall we imagine that body and still remain religious thinkers or imaginers? This is not an idle or a passing question. In fact, I am sure that there are many who will say that it happens to be precisely the central question of modern theology; it creates a threatening division between two great groups among Christians today. The activist, the radical, and the revolutionary tend to say that the detail of the metaphor and its location in human experience is the whole of the matter; the other half of the polarity tends to see this as an attack on the true religion of the living God.

Just like talk about God, *this* contemporary tendency to schism cannot be settled by one aphorism or cheap slogan but must be come at in a number of ways. If I may give a rough description of where I stand I repeat that everything I have ever written asks for the concrete movement of faith and the imagination through experience, through time, through the definite, through the human, through the actual life of Christ. This whole area must come to life as world of religion. Much of my work has been to try to persuade the mentally ill that this is the way the world works. But—and here some will stop reading—this position can develop its own arrogance, its own vicious lack of what I shall begin in a moment to call irony. I despise that arrogance of the concrete which is always demanding, as a movement and an ideology, that the world line up for or against it and is always willing to tear the Church apart in the name of its own prophetic authenticity. There is all the difference in the world between saying that faith must have a political embodiment and saying that this means men of faith have the final political answers. Much as I admire him and admire him as an ironist, there is something of this about Kierkegaard, something of the conviction that it is more important to be sincere and authentic than right. This is another form of that passionate and beautiful being Dionysus. We do need and must have activism, we can no longer accept passivity, but it will be the irony of faith itself that can alone prevent the revolution from falling, ironically, into a new clericalism and a religious fascism that will listen to no word in assembly but its own. For what it is worth they can have my head now. Though I would prefer first to finish this study of irony.

*   *   *

The best and fullest bibliography on the subject of the ironic imagination and irony in literature will be found in D. C. Muecke's *The Compass of Irony* (London, 1969). There is a shorter volume and a shorter bibliography by Muecke, called *Irony* (London, 1970), in the series *The Critical Idiom*.

Some of the most interesting of the books in English on irony are J. A. K. Thomson, *Irony: An Historical Introduction* (London, 1926), which is an excellent analysis of the formal beginnings of irony in the Greek and Latin writers; A. R. Thompson, *The Dry Mock, A Study of Irony in Drama* (Berkeley, 1948); M. L. Gurewitch, *European Romantic Irony* (Ann Arbor, 1962); Connor Thirlwall, "On the Irony of Sophocles," *The Philological Museum*, vol. 2 (Cambridge, 1833); E. E. Sedgwick, *Of Irony, Especially in Drama* (Toronto, 1948); Erich Heller, *The Ironic German* (Boston, 1958), an excellent and very readable study of the irony of Thomas Mann; Cleanth Brooks, "Irony as a Principle of Structure," in *Literary Opinion in America*, edited by Zabel, Morton, Dauwen (New York, 1951).

To try to recommend a list of great or important ironic authors and books would be an ambitious project, especially when we are told that the whole of the modern genius is ironic. At least we can mention the eminent ironists. There is the figure of Socrates and the dialogues of Plato; (it is amazing how little formal work has been done on Socratic irony). There are the plays of Sophocles.

There is of course *Don Quixote*. There is a study of "English Irony before Chaucer" in the *University of Toronto Quarterly* 6 (July, 1937), 538-557; The principal figures in Thompson's *The Dry Mock* are Tieck, Pirandello, Molière, Shaw, Aeschylus, Sophocles, Euripides, and Ibsen.

The novel *Lucinde* of Schlegel is one of the fountainheads of German romantic irony. Of Kierkegaard there is everything, but especially his dissertation *The Concept of Irony* and *Either/Or*. And the essay *L'humorismo* by Pirandello, as well as the plays. Apart from the novels there are the two significant short pieces by Thomas Mann, *Death in Venice* and *Tonio Kröger*. But these are a limited list of suggested explorations in the vast field of the modern ironic imagination. How that imagination is always ironically defeating the things we expect and the endings we expect is especially dealt with in Frank Kermode's *The Sense of an Ending* (Oxford, 1967).

*   *   *

The first thing we can say about faith's imagination is that it composes reality with irony and with ironic images.

Centrally I shall be meaning that irony deals not with appearances, but with the very opposite of appearances, and that its main task is to keep opposites together in a single act of the imagination. Thus if we ask the question, what is power? Who has the real power? Appearance will say the powerful have power, but the beatitudes and the sermon on the mount in the Gospel of St.

Matthew say the opposite. Like the imagination itself, faith moves below appearances into existence. In the primary sense of the word *metaphysical* they are both metaphysical.

*　　*　　*

Let me reflect on this question of the irony of co-existing opposites.

It is not ironic that any and every pair of opposites should coexist in the same individual or the same situation. For example, there is nothing at all ironic in the coexistence of the one and the many in the same subject. This is a contrariety that is not only ordinary but that is essential to the existence of anything. Also it is a contrariety that can be explained and rationalized. It belongs completely to the life of reason. In *The Parmenides* Plato worked out a remarkably long and complicated set of contraries that must belong to any unit thing in the world. He was not being ironic, though A. E. Taylor and Paul Elmer More said he was.

Nor is there anything ironic about contradiction, though this may very well be the understanding that many people have of irony: the co-presence of contradictory elements. I agree with the unfriendly position of Karl Popper toward contradiction, namely that the only thing to do with it is to clear it up and get rid of it.

No, the usual quality of irony is the unexpected coexistence, to the point of identity, of certain contraries. Usually the words *contraries* and *contrariety* are employed in a metaphysical sense. The philosophical understanding is that contraries come in pairs and the pairs in each case are the two most widely separated members of the one species or class, or the two most widely separated subspecies. Thus the very hot and the very cold are the contraries within the situations referred to by the word *temperature*. The very mad and the very wise among mankind would be a pair of contraries and a contrariety that begins to be metaphysical. They are the most widely separated. But suddenly we realize, ironically, that in man, and in one and the same man, they are not widely separated.

The shock of irony (and of recognition) comes not only from uniting them but also from seeing that the act of uniting them is not a mistake. Thus through the book-long pairing of Don Quixote and Sancho Panza the whole novel is ironic. In philosophy not only the method but the very physical figure of Socrates is ironic because it is the ugliest of men who is producing the most beautiful of thoughts. In Christianity there is more than fascinating coexistence of the low and the high. The lowliness is the very instrument to be passed through in order to reach the high. It is also right to say that it *is* the high. And there is more than paradox or ironic brilliance involved. There is an actual transformation of being. For those who, at least at heart, are spiritually free of this world's enormous goods possess forms of real power and freedom.

*   *   *

In the pre-Christian world it is Socrates who in philosophy becomes the synonym for irony and pays for the gift with his life. Even physically he is the model of irony. For he is an ugly man from whom beautiful things come forth. He is always saying nothing at all, he minimizes his knowledge but will not retract it. Reversely he goes around the Athenian marketplace demonstrating that those who think they know really do not know anything. It is the ugly and the ignorant Socrates who becomes the founder of Western culture and science. What more ironic than this? The worldly Alcibiades pays him supreme tribute in *The Symposium*.

There he is, Socrates, at the beginning of our history, an extraordinary summary of what we began to be and still are. It is hard to think of another who so much sums up our mental and physical life. A combination of endless irony, brilliance, *and* moral seriousness. A *love of ugliness* as a way of saying beautiful things. He wanted to put everything to the test of the critical intelligence. But he believed that one thing was not another; to say this was the most remarkable act of the mind, and the heart of the doctrine of Ideas. He is the most flexible and ironic man in Athens, and the most committed. He is strong enough to be absolutely ironic. He is completely calm in the political order but cannot manage his wife. He is the permanent ironic hero of Western civilization.

*   *   *

Yet his enemies were on the verge of being right. The charge against him, that he made the worse appear the better reason, was wrong. In fact he picked reasons and he died for them. And the fact that he went about showing men they did not know what they were talking about is only the reverse of that coin by which he founded definition, objectivity, discernment, ratio, knowing what we are talking about. But he did have the gift of proving anything and everything, the brilliant gift by which thought is becoming brilliantly conscious of its own suppleness and beauty. Thought was becoming capable of dissolving anything into its opposite. Irony and the ironic imagination *can* dissolve everything. At least certain forms of irony can.

Socrates was great enough to be a constant and powerful ironist. But when smaller people adopt the complete life of irony it is a far more dangerous game. I do not think it is possible to detect meanness or malice in the irony of Socrates. But the irony of lesser people can be both mean and malicious. The images of irony they produce are often mean and miserable creations of contempt, full of salvation for no one.

*   *   *

But who more ironic, in terms of coexisting opposites, than Pascal, the external style of whose *Pensées* I distantly imitate? "What sort of freak then is man! How novel, how monstrous, how chaotic, how paradoxical, how prodigious! Judge of all things, feeble earthworm, repository of truth, sink of doubt and error, glory and refuse of the universe!"

In these speculations he had the remarkable gift, not of painting what he knows to be contradictions, nor of dissolving what seem to be contradictions, but of letting stand, each as a fact, what cannot be put together by the mind: " . . . there are in faith two equally constant truths. One is that man in the state of his creation, or in the state of grace, is exalted above the whole of nature, made like unto God and sharing in his divinity. The other is that in the state of corruption and sin he has fallen from the first state and become like the beasts."[2]

*   *   *

Some of the central contrarieties in the interior life of Christian faith are immediately evident. There are the promises of Christ and the death of Christ. There are the great thoughts, the great visions, the great promises, the great things that are here and are to come. Eye hath not seen, nor ear heard. Then there are the common human thoughts, the extremely common human feelings, the common human tasks and needs, as though—if one chose to put it that way and if one *chose* that brand of irony—as though this second world were laughing and mocking at the first. There is the part that thinks divine thoughts, almost without limit; there is the other part that is weakness itself and that shall die.

It is necessary that there be a very close relationship and friendship between these two parts of man, so much so that it will be disastrous for either if it gets separated from the other. If we go about thinking only great thoughts in the name of faith, forgetting the human, we become mad dreamers, fanatical human beings, ruthless, absolutizers, destroying and not redeeming the human. The human, in its weakness, needs the companionship and redemption of faith. And faith seems more able to give this companionship and understanding than the pure intelligence. For the pure intelligence is more apt to wish to rise above the human condition and to despise the latter. But the most special concern of faith is redemption, the redemption of the parts of man that need to be redeemed.

This does not mean that faith becomes identified with weakness, loses its own nobility, becomes indolent, accepts the status quo. If there is a friendship between faith and the human, the best and final consequence should be that this friendship become externalized and objectified and universalized. There should be a steady relationship, to the point of passion, between faith and the poor, between faith and Africa, Asia. But that will not happen unless there is first this interior and originating contrariety in which faith loves its own interior and poor humanity.

In the images of faith the images of personal redemption and social justice cannot be separated.

*   *   *

So the opposites must at all cost be held together. We can never separate the inner and the outer. The revolutionary cannot in the process destroy his own soul.

In the long line of attempts to rectify injustice in the *Oresteia* of Aeschylus—in all the attempts of human beings to act in the name of the justice of Zeus—there is always the ambiguity of a new and inward sin: of vengeance, self-righteousness, pride, arrogance or a new injustice. Thus the despairs of endlessness. It is part of the genius of Aeschylus to have imagined, by all the means at the disposal of the writer, this endlessness of guilt and injustice.

Apparently Dionysus did not even recognize the predicament. The seeming endlessness remains the fundamental problem of the radical and the revolutionary. They must remember, to their consolation, that there have been solutions. What were they? Who were they?

*   *   *

This is the way one Christian puts one phase of the problem:

] 89 [

We are not witnesses to just any justice, but to evangelical justice; that is where our sights should certainly be set. If not, we could be swept toward the ambiguous solutions of a human justice which is obscured by sin and often turned in on itself.

What then is the root of justice according to the Gospel? It is necessary to respond that justice which is sanctity is the root foundation of social justice: one gives rise to the other. Nothing is holy if it is not just; nothing is fully just that is not seeking holiness. Therefore, the love of God and of neighbor are inseparably united.

From this flow several consequences.

1. The action necessary to change political structures cannot replace the transformation of people; conversion of heart is indispensable.

2. The Christian cannot accept class struggle as the sole means for the transformation of the world. He must examine with equal care the way of law, of non-violent action, of love. Justice must be a progress toward liberty in charity. History shows us that exclusively human justice based on power creates hardship for men, especially when it becomes a political regime. It does not change hearts, it does not liberate men: it reigns over rebels. [Cardinal Roy, at the Synod, Rome, 1971]

It is also within this area and problematic of the spirit that the intellectual frequently makes his mistake. For he demonstrates too often, as a man of the left, that he does not hesitate to use the tactics of the right.

*   *   *

I begin to see in how many ambivalent forms faith makes its appearance and sets up its tent (tabernacles) among us. It is ironic that it feeds so strongly on nothingness and death. It is ironic that it should be in such a dynamic partnership with fear. It is ironic that it be in the constant company of whole sets of ordinary feelings which can be dealt with and lived with but never removed. If this were not so, faith itself would probably take on a Dionysian form and fury, so beautiful and so exalted, so intense and so powerful, so fair a creature among the ugly works of man, that it would be or become intolerable, and that would be the last and the worst irony of all. There have been forms of faith like this that have broken loose from all human mooring and partnership and have leaped into vast apocalyptic images, desires and actions.

Dionysus, I have said, is a fair young god who without the company of reason and the human is at one moment divine and in the next diabolical. Norman Cohn in his *The Pursuit of the Millenium* and Ronald Knox in his *Enthusiasm* both give extremely readable accounts of brilliant or mad episodes of such high-flown faith, unmodified by the simple ironies of the human spirit.[3]

Only if the human part of faith can assert itself against *this* enthusiasm, only if it can assert its own rights, only then can it turn on itself and create its own enthusiasm and its own prophecy, its own strength, its own irony. But if it does not begin by standing up to the false prophets and by asserting itself against their universal irony, then it is licked before it begins. It must take this risk even if in the doing and the taking it does not feel holy and in fact feels not admirable.

*   *   *

Now how keep fear and faith together in an image of faith?

Thus Luther himself was very careful not to make too decisive a separation between the fear of God and filial confidence in God. He has a very fascinating way of recognizing a double life in faith. There is a faith in the fidelity of the mercy of God. But faith is also fear, which has its roots in the sanctity of God. The faith which is confidence will win out over the fear, but will not seek to suppress the latter. Confidence will finally triumph, but with fear and trembling. And it will be a triumph of faith against faith (*fide contra fidem*).[4]

I see nothing particularly wonderful in my almost recommending the continuing presence of fear, other than that it is a fact of Christian consciousness and not an unholy distortion of it. And here is a marvelous seeing of the fear that is part of us as part of a proper image of faith. This is infinitely better than that we be told, hypocritically, that we must live an unreal and impossible inward life and that a true Christian does not fear. By the complete rejection of fear, such an apostle of "pure" faith creates this kind of inward life for us, and creates more absolutes than he is trying to avoid. He at one moment gives us absolute fear and in the next absolute faith. But one cannot concoct one true image out of two false images of faith.

Therefore, it seems right to say that the structure of the irony of faith is not marked by a temporal sequence of the ironic elements but by the simultaneous presence of contraries.

*   *   *

The image of faith never separates out the good and the bad.

It is very important that the faith and the incredulity in this body of faith be not separated out into two acts that have forgotten each other. The relations of the two should be after the model of the operation of the same and the different in the idea of being. All the things "that are" are the same and different; but the same cannot be sorted out from the different. Let that be the case with belief and unbelief. Otherwise what happens is that we will believe only in the ideal and only mock the present reality. Thus illusion and reality, faith and unfaith, will be neatly compartmentalized. This would represent an enormous oversimplification of the actual forms of sensibility that have been built up by history as part of the body of faith. Anybody can believe in the ideal; it is no great trick at all, and takes no effort. (It will be right for the child to so begin). What is necessary is that we come with faith and unfaith, with a sense of reality and illusion, belief and criticism, high seriousness and mockery, to the same reality in the one and same act. There are those who want to separate out the two into two different acts, two different camps, two different realities, two different Churches. But what is proposed in the present hour of the crisis of faith and of society? Nothing less than that an ideal people should form an underground church, the church of the idea.

Freedom of association is an inviolable right but we must ask what are the good and the bad reasons for going apart. Dietrich Bonhoeffer and so many others were right when they formed a truly Confessing Church to fight the Nazis, but he came to suspect he was wrong in declaring this group to be the true Church. It seems to be the teaching of Christ that good and bad must stay together until the final judgment. Imagine the horror of separating out the good in this life.

*   *   *

Parody and mockery, a certain refusal to "believe," can be part of many forms of real belief and seriousness. Very many of the most beautiful works of man are the result of such an ironic combination of qualities and styles. It is as though man is immensely helped if he does these two things together; mock at things and himself and take things and himself very seriously. Something like this is being chosen as the unique style of the Christian man and artist by Erich Auerbach in *Mimesis*. Again it is the double style of the low and the high.

* * *

The Representation of Reality in Western Literature is the secondary title of Auerbach's book, which remains one of the classics of modern criticism. The human reality is at its very heart ironic, being both a shocking and a marvelous composition of high and low, but the antique style and almost law of classical literature had commanded the separation of the two worlds of the common and the sublime. These walls are crumbling decisively in the Old Testament: "from the very first, in the Old Testament stories, the sublime, tragic, and problematic take shape precisely in the domestic and commonplace. . . ." But if this is true of the whole Hebraic tradition it is even more astonishingly true of every occurrence in the New Testament: "these occurrences on the plane of everyday life assume the importance of world-revolutionary events, as later on they will for everyone."[5]

Surely there must be a sturdy relation between the new mixed images of faith and the vast realistic and ironic achievements that developed and are still developing in the history of Western literature. There has been a great emergence of the common and even of the random as the seat of the tragic and of the important.

*   *   *

There can be no *a priori* and philosophical definition of the irony in the ironic image of faith. It must be the irony of Christ, but as this means Chirst in all his particularity, *this* irony could not have been either pre-determined or predefined. This irony is a special.and (to put it mildly) imaginative intervention in the turbulent, pre-existing, sometimes mad history of the ironies of faith.

Let me remember this as I now make bold to suggest that there are certain general features in every success-fully ironic image or composition of faith. I repeat that a frequent quality of the ironic situation is a fruitful relationship of what I have called the larger and the smaller line in the ironic situation. Sometimes the larger line in the universe simply overwhelms the smaller. The simplest secular example I think of is an architectural one, where the large, same, repetitive inhuman line in a great housing development has no room for detail or difference. The large line wins an easy victory for its rough, obvious ironies. On the other hand, a reason why again and again we call someone imaginative is that he has so imagined detail that it not only survives but shines forth in the composition.

Christ himself in his particularity is the final model for the successful relationship of the smaller and the greater line. Against the background of enormous space time, at a completely specific and free moment in the millions of light years, within a body that occupies a few feet of the space of all our universes, he seizes upon and declares importance and seriousness, his own. This is ironic, that this should happen at an infinitely small point in infinitely large space time. It is, in a completely literal way, the basic image of faith. I hope it is not blasphemous to say that it took imagination.

*   *   *

One of the forces that is always in the position of overwhelming the definiteness of historical events is the archetypal image. In archetypal thinking it is the mighty human spirit which by itself breeds the idea of God, of the Judge, of Love, of Might, of the Great Mother, of the Son of God.

What does the archetype care for any moment of history or any event? It spawns all Scriptural events out of its own great maw, its own overwhelming infinity. The event thinks it is an event; it thinks that something has happened; but the archetype solemnly declares that nothing has happened, that it has spawned all these endless imitations of itself, including Christ. The particular is but an insignificant illustration of the archetype's great formula. The archetype is arrogant; the archetype must be unmasked; apart from history and reality it would starve in a day; it must be stood up to. It is like that faith of a child or that faith of Medea which is huge, wild, unformed, blind, and must be educated by people and events. (My view of the unconscious comes closer to the realistic picture of that wild, unformed and not magnificent unconscious that we are given by Freud, than to that romantic, dreaming, all-generating abyss which we are given by Jung and which

I with many others question.) There is no need of history yielding to this young monster. History must not yield to *its* infinite contempts, boredom, furies, ironies, its assaults on event and history.

History must grapple with the beastie, and must fight back with its own ironies. Why must we bow to the power and the beauty of this unconscious? I think that the power and beauty of faith or imagination depends on a progressive relationship with reality, history, and revelation. Otherwise faith remains a permanent child. And I do not see how we solve anything by declaring that there is not only a psychoanalytic unconscious, there is also a religious unconscious. The unconscious becomes religious through education. This does not mean that the unconscious is not a vast and mighty depth. That it is precisely this is my first assumption. But it is a blind and mighty child. A Dionysus. When, therefore, I assign a temporal priority to faith in the faith-knowledge sequence it is not in order to restore the priority of the *Homo Religiosus* and the religious instinct according to the pictures the great Protestant theologians, beginning with Schleiermacher, had created in the nineteenth century.

*   *   *

But we often theorize ourselves into submission and yield to the pressures of contemporary discussion before there is real need. It is partly because of an intellectual fascism in the air that we conclude so quickly that there must be a split between the new world of space and time and the world of biblical images. What can so small and definite a set of images, and so narrow and given a history have to do with the new magnificence?

It may help us to remember that everything within this large world lives within its own world, and knows the large world only through its own. Nothing, no one, just plain lives "within the universe." It is impossible so to live. We live within the language of our bodies, receiving upon them and within their terms the impact of the universe. We live within the language of *a* language, using its miniscule forms to describe the universe. The language of science is number, measurement, calculus, to describe the world; despite its achievement and despite the grandeur of its object, it is still a very *limited* language-world performing a great task. The great universe depends on all these narrow languages and objectifications to elucidate it. Here is the Hebraic-Christian image. Within this language too we read the world.

* * *

It is the mark of an elite group to claim that it alone knows the meaning of words, it alone has the true faith, it alone is on the inside of things. If there are many forms of irony—many forms of language in which words say more than they seem or say the opposite of their seeming—this is the special irony of the elite, to declare that they alone are on the inside of words and things. This kind of irony is often used to create a sense of identity; it marks people off from the everyday run of people. (Only the masses will accept the ordinary meaning). It is clear that it is divisive. It does not *pass through* a lesser or literal meaning to get to a higher. It refuses to pass through the smaller line. It translates the lesser or the lower or the literal away; it is cabalistic and secret. It does not give any real power to the lower to move into the higher meaning. It does not want to move through the lower, but to transcend it. Secretly, therefore, it has no use for the human and is never really funny. It rejects that fundamental act of the imagination which is passage through reality. For such an elite there is no real relationship, in their images of faith, between the smaller and the larger line. In the past they have also usually shown themselves as fearful of historical fact and event.

*   *   *

Another such collapse of the structure of the ironic image occurs in boredom.

One of the greatest temptations of the ironic imagination is boredom. It is actually one of the great forms of irony. It is, but in reverse, as great a force as faith. Where faith, for good or bad, is a tremendous drive toward relationship and contains all the energies that we associate with the life of wishing and longing, boredom moves in just the opposite way. If I may speak ironically and, I hope, not too cleverly—for irony very easily does just that—boredom is a tremendous force for not wishing. I think we give part of its secret away when we reveal it as a force for not wishing. The bored man is acting, within faith, in an intense way which says: I do not wish; I do not want this, I do not want that, unto infinity. I am not impressed by this event or that, by this image or that. Mention any event and I shall wipe it out. Do not try to impress me for I am not vulnerable. And do not tell me that I am not impressed by religious images; I am impressed by no images. I do not wish to be impressed.

*   *   *

To work out a new irony is a difficult and never-ending task. In the centuries since Christ, it had to and did lead to a complete democratization of the image of man and to the impossibility of any theology built upon class or race or nation; all these categories were destroyed by this overwhelming idea of men as sons of God; but once the categories were destroyed as ultimates, it was possible to breathe new life back into them; they in their turn can now master irony, so that a Christian can be what he is and wishes. But they all remain under constant judgment and reformation. Man's work or role or function is no longer his substance as eternally established in a rigid class system; that taken for granted, the elements of human difference become manageable images of faith.

Over against the vast irony of the universe, which seems to negate human action and to bring it under contempt, there is the frightening insertion of value in the smallest human action. There is a tenacious struggle for the law of God in the human area. There is the threat of Christ that all will be paid for, down to the last farthing. The detail is important.

But now the pendulum has swung again. The image of the world has grown larger and larger against the possibility of human action. The images of the world are becoming more and more excited. The images are in a state of alarm. All the Systems have become unmanageable. Whatever the reality, they are seen as threatening the smaller lines.

*   *   *

Some time ago I wrote a study of comedy.[6] A good deal of its method was to try to distinguish what I conceived to be the true comic spirit from many other spirits that might resemble it but that in fact were its very opposites. Comedy involves an extraordinarily close, factual, and sympathetic imagining of the human condition. But there are many comic spirits that have nothing but hatred or contempt for the human condition.

So again with irony. One irony is not another. Irony moves all the way from the Spirit of Christ to the spirit of pure evil. The irony of Christ is unique. It involves the mastery of the world, spiritual freedom, freedom from the past and from every form of that which imprisons; it works through death and weakness; it therefore dethrones every other pretentious idea and establishes the movement through the human condition, and total human condition (not the human condition of the beautiful people) as the way. Weakness becomes one of the great forms of power. Age, sickness, and death lose their power over man and take on another form of power. Precisely what we are becomes the ironic mode of transcendence of what we are.

*   *   *

I do not intend to define irony in one step. It is better to grow into our definitions.

One of the ways by which the power and energy of faith are controlled, shaped, and directed is by irony and all its related instincts (parody, mockery, humor, contempt, etc.). In fact irony must not exist on the outside of faith, but must get into the very heart of faith. When effectively and properly present it is a part of faith itself. For we can say either one of two things.

Either we can say that left to itself faith believes too much and too indiscriminately, believing everything, absolutizing everything (this is the faith that leads to disappointment, despair and fury); irony comes along to educate faith. Or we can say that the irony which knows how to de-absolutize things and control belief is faith itself.

Irony has many forms; in general I think of it as the negative principle in faith (negation is very important). This negative principle is not necessarily a cool, deliberate, calculating, lucid, intellectual thing. It can be and is as full of power and passion as the positive principle in belief. Faith without irony can lead to fury. But if irony is separated out from faith and comes to lead its own independent existence, it not only becomes a principle of universal mockery; it destroys everything; it becomes diabolical. It not only wipes out false gods, it wipes out everything. It declares that *nothing* is of *any* importance. And since it is more than an intellectual force, its violent, explosive passion can shake the world. Only faith itself, only the restoration of the sense of the important and the serious, can handle it.

Therefore a very usual circular rhythm in life is this: Faith goes blindly and independently about until it discovers the guide of irony. Irony (or mockery) breaks out into autonomy and needs the guide of faith. We shall watch some of the interactions of these two principles in the sensibility of faith.

*　　*　　*

The pleasure of the diabolical is intense and complete. It is the joy of evil. This joy in evil is a common pleasure, known by all. A purely independent irony, or contempt, is an absolute pleasure. Is there a joy in this world as great as the joy of evil? This is a thing we do not talk about. We go around proclaiming that only the good are happy, that the evil are miserable. This is not true. I go back to Medea to see that she is really enjoying herself. The thing we do not talk about is that the absolute defiance of the good and of God is an absolute joy. It is an irony that wishes to stand completely apart from any reality.

Irony can be magnificent. It can also involve a failure of nerve.

*   *   *

The ironical and the dialectical cannot accept "things-as-they-are" and both have a double vision of reality. They cannot accept the one-dimensional man or thing. The term "one-dimensional," can cover a whole spectrum of situations from the pure given fact of empiricism to the social given called the status quo.

Neither can I accept the one-dimensional man, and I too accept the need of double vision. What a revolutionary philosopher (Herbert Marcuse) is saying in the following is that we cannot accept the single, unchangeable vision of things-as-they-are and that things-as-they-are must be subject to thought and criticism. Though it is fascinating to see how his image of this judgmental task of thought becomes that of subversion:

> . . . that which is cannot be true." To our well-trained ears and eyes, this statement is flippant and ridiculous, or as outrageous as that other statement which seems to say the opposite: "what is real is rational." And yet, in the tradition of Western

thought, both reveal, in provocatively abridged formulation, the idea of Reason which has guided its logic. Moreover, both express the same concept, namely, the antagonistic structure of reality, and of thought trying to understand reality. The world of immediate experience—the world in which we find ourselves living—must be comprehended, transformed, even subverted in order to become that which it really is.

In the equation Reason = Truth = Reality, which joins the subjective and objective world into one antagonistic unity, Reason is the subversive power, the "power of the negative" that establishes, as theoretical and practical Reason, the truth for men and things—that is, the conditions in which men and things become what they really are.[7]

* * *

Here is another putting of the case by the same writer as he refuses to accept "things-as-they-are." There must be a double vision of things-as-they-are.

... the subversive character of truth inflicts upon thought an *imperative* quality. Logic centers on judgments which are, as demonstrative propositions, imperatives,—the predicate "is" implies *"ought"*.

This contradictory, two-dimensional style of thought is the inner form not only of dialectical logic but of all philosophy which comes to grips with reality. The propositions which define reality affirm as true something that is *not* (immediately) the case; thus they contradict that which is the case, and they deny its truth.[8]

This is dialectical thought. It offers itself as an attack

on every form of one-dimensional thought. It demands the double image, the one critical of the other. The *ought* is critical of the *is*.

* * *

But suppose the ought—as the larger line—becomes completely separated from the *is?*

By insisting on the prior necessity of absolute destruction and the great refusal, and by declining to offer any specific plan or substitute for the present immediacy, the present illusion, revolution without imagination executes a brilliant maneuver. It avoids being caught in that human round of idea-and-specificity which in turn invites refusal, mockery, disbelief. What is avoided is the new immediacy of some, any, absolutely present moment. Such a dialectic indeed reduces reality to a pure *ought*. This is as good a definition as any for the nature of moral absolutism. The *is* is not modified by *ought*. It is replaced by it. In the face of such an overpowering *ought,* all reality is reduced to an illusion and there is faith in nothing. You do not have to think in two ways. The *ought* becomes the single clear idea. This is the irony of all revolution separated from imagination: it becomes one-dimensional and thereby joins the very thing it criticizes. And it becomes absolute puritanism.

Therefore there is sense in the recent French battle cry: *the revolution to the imagination.* The radical and the revolutionary have a profound obligation to live the life of the imagination. The first consequence would be to transform the revolution into many revolutions. Revolution in what?

Dialectical thought can destroy itself as often as it becomes so intense and absolute that the ought wipes out every possible *is* and every possible smaller line. I repeat my point—which is now a new irony—that such absolutizing wipes out the gap and itself becomes one-dimensional. The pure ought has no faith in anything but the pure idea. And it rejects the work of the imagination.

*   *   *

Nevertheless we are here faced with the serious question of our day. Crane Brinton puts it well.[9] We used to be very tolerant of the gap between is and ought. But how tolerant of how big a gap can we be today?

The right kind of sensibility cannot be produced overnight. It needs training and criticism and self-awareness. It especially needs to be aware of its own rhetoric and hollowness, as often as this is the case. Otherwise it can produce nothing but clichés, fashionable disgust, automated ecstasy. Such irony is chockful of self-righteousness. This is not because it is ironic but because it does not go far enough; it is not sufficiently ironic. This is the fundamental weakness in the technical workmanship of much of what might be called the new irony in the new culture, that its irony is operating only on a surface level that will lead, ironically, to self-betrayal.

How so?

The self-betrayal consists in building into its satiric and savagely critical images (how could we live without them and their fun and truth) an incredible image of its own beauty. Structurally it has separated out this beauty from the remainder of redeemable humanity.

This claim to beauty is the assumption which leaves it completely vulnerable. I have suggested the dangers and the reasons for criticism of a uniquely apocalyptic view of Christianity. Now it is just in this direction, of the apocalyptic, that the new culture commits an error which it must learn how to correct from modern irony itself. If we examine an enormous accumulation of images in music, film and drama, both American and English (for example, *Easy Rider, Joe, Little Big Man, If, The Charge of the Light Brigade, Zabriskie Point, The Living Theatre, Hair, The Graduate, Dr. Strange-love, Woodstock, Catch-22, A Clockwork Orange, Sticks and Bones, The Discreet Charm of the Bourgeoisie*, etc.) this claim to its own beauty and this threat of eternal destruction for its enemies is clear.

*   *   *

If the intellectual does not master these crucial, these central ironies, if he does not solve the problem of the creation of the right irony, then he will find himself cut off from the very classes to whom he wishes to be so close, and will be forced in on a more and more intense and exclusive companionship with his own kind, that is to say: with the intellectuals. This is indeed what has happened and what is happening. I agree with those who believe that the intellectuals are becoming a social class, preoccupied with themselves, living in the minds of one another, and this is most unfortunate. For the intelligence is healthiest when two things are true of it; when it is related to human society and when, paradoxically enough, it is acting with independent integrity and autonomy. But when the intellectuals begin to be increasingly turned in on themselves (no longer the teachers of society) and when they react with increasing uniformity, predictability, and rigidity to every issue, then they are in sore trouble. And that they have developed such an intense sociological need of each other can only be a source of interference with intellectual independence. I think therefore that they have more to fear from each other than from the political order or the middle class. They should fear each other with a great, with almost a biblical fear. We need their independence.

4: The Images of Faith and Human Time

MAN IS A TEMPORAL, HISTORICAL BEING WHO IS TO BE UNDER-stood and defined in relation to the internal time scheme he occupies, from his birth to his death. This is his essence and it is only by seeing this that we will escape the quarrel between the essentialists and the dramatists. And it is by traveling back and forth in certain highly developed ways along the lines of human and Christic time that he lives the life of faith, by memory, by action, and by hope. Nothing less even begins to define what faith is.

Let us try, therefore, to do two things.

Let us try to understand and define man temporally, according to the moving structure and rhythm of the time stages through which he passes from birth to death.

Let us do the same thing, *pari passu*, for faith. Let us understand it temporally, seizing as best we can its own movement, its history, its growth, its education. For it too has a story and a definition in terms of a story.

Let us watch faith imagining and experiencing this world, not statically, not all in a moment, not by instantaneous epiphany, but according to the movement and stages of life.

*　　*　　*

History, too, is paradigm, a way of experiencing facts.

But one does not have facts or experience first, and then compose them within a history. We cannot denominate a single historical fact without first of all having a history within which alone the fact has name, identity, and existence. Thus, according to which way you want to look at it, the single fact is contained within a whole history, or contains the thought structure of a whole history. Who was George Washington? He was first president of the United States.

A Christian is one who locates himself mentally and rememberingly within the Judaic-Christian line of history and proposes to interpret experience with the help of that part of history. The Eucharist and Liturgy is a formal, solemn, public and dramatic reminder of this historical identity. This is surely part of the meaning of the central phrase: "Do this in memory of me." Thus the Eucharist is not only a commemoration and reenactment of a historical event, it is also a commemoration of who, historically, I am. It seems to me that if identity has this strong historical character then we are well on the way toward canceling any great dichotomy between historical Christianity and its present existential meaning in human Heideggerian terms of relevancy.

But history is alive and growing. It needs me as much as I need it. There is a back and forth between me and history.

* * *

Faith, I repeat, should be able to move in its images between the past, the present, and the future. In this sense it is basically and continuously historical and dramatic. The present image is packed with the past and the future. This makes the images of faith not less but more human, for this is the way the human imagination acts when at its most active best, dramatically. Faith therefore makes the imagination take on an extremely active and not a passive role. But let us look at the purely human plane first to see what is involved when the imagination is active and dramatic. It moves along the line of time in a very complicated way.

1. Childhood

Let us watch faith in its first stage.

The faith of the child is absolute; that is its strength and its weakness. If we were to hypothesize that the child doubts, we should also have to hypothesize that the child would despair. If the promises made to him by his single source of nature are broken, if the mother willy-nilly breaks the promises, we shall see how terrible the results can be. A shift of ground, a thrust of flexibility in another direction, a change of perspective, a falling back upon inner resource, a decision to wait, a managing to make a molehill out of a mountain—all are as yet impossible. Work like that of the French psychologist Piaget has helped us to understand in further detail how much the child absolutizes in all his thinking and feeling. This mother is the whole of reality; this feeling is the whole of the emotional life; this single perspective is the whole of the mountain; this adult figure is almighty God himself. But when knowledge and feeling begin to be more relative they also begin to be more educated, more mature. So too with faith. Because it is faith that I am interested in, I am saying that it is faith that must be educated, especially if it is so strong.

*   *   *

Let me continue to reconstruct the sheer power and energy that is carved into a human being from the first moment of existence by the form of faith and unfaith. In the following description of a child, seven and a half months old, whose mother has been removed from her, let us imagine, as is indeed the case, that promises have first been made to the child by the mother, that the enormous energy of a flow of trust has been elicited, and that for some reason or other that energy has been betrayed; the loved object that by gesture, sound, and feeling had made the promises is no longer there. We are watching what happens when another of these primal forms of faith, perhaps the most fundamental, goes away.

She lay immobile in her crib. When approached she did not lift her shoulders, barely her head, to look at the experimenter with an expression of profound suffering sometimes seen in sick animals. With this expression she examined the observer. As soon as another observer started to speak to her or to touch her she began to weep. This was not the usual crying of babies which is always accompanied by a certain amount of vocalization, going into screaming. It was a soundless weeping, tears running down her face. Speaking to her in soft comforting tones only resulted in the weeping becoming more intense, intermingled with moans and sobs, shaking her whole body.[1]

*   *   *

What we might call the childhood forms of faith and the corresponding forms of the imagination are quite various, but all these forms have certain common and very recognizable characteristics. One of them is a passion not only for fantasy but for decisive fantasy.

The results can be humanly various. There is nothing as charming as the world the child builds in such play. But what must his images be in the case, on the one hand, of those in whom he has faith and, on the other, those in whom he does not believe? It is in the one case a land of beautiful people, of soft skin and lovely hair, innocent, perfect, large, most competent and good; over against them is the other tribe, the monsters, the big teeth, the wicked eye, the dirty hair, the threatening aspect. The world becomes divided, with an incredible rationality and perfectionism of images, into the good people and the bad people. Apparently the same process goes further. There is a good mother with a beautiful face and a bad mother with a horrible face. Everything is clear, nothing is left in doubt. There is no irony.

One must remember that this is a brilliant and fascinating world. It will always be attractive. And as our world begins with these great childhood images of good and evil and the bright and the dark, so we are told by a later faith that the cosmos itself will end on such a clear, heroic note, with the bright and the dark divided, separated from one another, but that in the meantime things must stay more mixed. The great childhood forms of the imagination and of faith are prophetic, but in the meantime—for the many stages of history and experience that must intervene between the beginning and the end—they are not yet truth but prophecies.

But in America today the prophecies are invading the reality. And there are vast residual images of childhood faith abroad, in the mutual images of the culture classes.

*　　*　　*

I seize the moment to share my late discovery of a magnificent book written fifty years ago: F. J. Harvey

Darton's *Children's Books in England, Five Centuries of Social Life.* It is indeed a perfect case of better late than never. Those who know say it is the best of the books on children's books, and it is a witty and wonderful review of five centuries of our trying to tackle, handle, understand, educate, and distort the imagination of the child. Here one can read all about it, with ease and pleasure and concretion. The first sentence sets the tone: "By children's books I mean printed works produced ostensibly to give children spontaneous pleasure, and not primarily to teach them, nor solely to make them good, not to keep them *profitably* quiet."

There is Aesop, there is the *Gesta Romanorum,* there are the romances of the Middle Ages; there is Robin Hood, the great hero of Sherwood Forest ("as soon as books were printed for children, he leapt into them"); there was Bevis (who "as a child was sold by a wicked mother to the Saracens"); then the Bestiaries ("In Araby there are many camelions, that is a little beast, and never eateth or drinketh, and he changeth his colour often, for sometimes he is of one colour, and sometimes of another, and he may change him into all colours that he will, save black or red"—it may paradoxically be pointed out here that most adults believe, too indiscriminately, that camelions change their colors and spots into *all* colors, but in this case children believe with more accuracy); there was the literature of the Puritans ("The authors wrote to the end that children might be saved from hell" . . . "the tormented logic and arbitrary creed of full Puritanism"); the fairies and the little people ("The Robin Goodfellows, elves, fairies, hobgoblins of our later age, did most of their pranks by night"—from Nash); "The fear or dislike of fairy tales, in fact . . . is a manifestation, in England, of a deep rooted sin-complex. It involves the belief that anything fantastic on the one hand, or anything primitive on the other, is inherently noxious or at least so void of good as to be actively dangerous."

But I shall never get to Robinson Crusoe, to Charles and Mary Lamb, to Edward Lear, to William Blake, to Alice in Wonderland. So I shall stop. But not before citing Darton's tribute to the Victorians:

> [Now] children could go back to the enchantments of the Middle Ages without being told that they were the work of the Devil; to Aesop and traveller's tales with the knowledge that such fables were not true but were thoroughly worthy of belief and love; to folk-lore with open rapture in the rogueries of the Booted Cat and the decapitation of ogres, without any warnings about superstition or ignorance or unreality; to fun, without being told not to be silly. And, say what you will, *Holiday House, The Book of Nonsense, Tom Brown, Sing-Song, The Water Babies, At the Back of the North Wind* were pure "Victorian" products and nothing else. Not only did no other age invent them; no other age could have invented them.[2]

*   *   *

For all those who do not have time to move with any leisure through the endless world of children's literature, the child's imagination, and the child's belief but would, with fascination, if they could, there are other alternatives and shortcuts. One of them would be to take up a good index and use it in a lively, active way, letting the titles set the imagination to work and now and then comparing the results with the actual text. For example, I take Mary Hirse Eastman's *Index to Fairy Tales, Myths and Legends,* of 606 pages (there is a supplementary volume of 562 pages) and register some of the titles, with but a few interfering remarks.[3] The first title still seems the best of all.

How many beans make five
How all things began
How Brother Fox was too smart
How cats came to purr
How crows became black
How King Midas lost his ears
How mosquitoes came
How sense was distributed
How summer came to earth
How Silver Fox created the world.

> *[You do not ask the question:* did *Fox create the world? For that is not the question. The question is:* how *did he do it?]*

How the bees got their sting
How the camel unbent

> *[There are twenty-five pages for the word* How, *an indication of the highly speculative and etiological nature of this imagination.]*

How the turkey got his beard
Land of discontented children
Land of Nod
Land of the dead
Land of youth
Old Lady of the forest
Old Lady's long leather bag
Old man's treachery
Why there are no snakes in Ireland
Why there are no snakes in Takhoma

[I had always believed that there were no snakes in Ireland but only a child could believe that there are no snakes in Takhoma.]

Witches' cellar

Zeus

[There is only this single entry under Zeus. It is followed by the imperious command "see Jupiter." This seems to mean that any fool knows there is no Zeus but there certainly is a Jupiter. However, there is no indication what a Jupiter is. The only difficulty with this whole book, one child complained, is that it has no index. But another explained that that is taken care of under the entry: How an infinite regress cannot, except in Takhoma, come to be. Most children believe this too about Takhoma (believing almost anything about the place) and in this they are supported by St. Thomas, who says that an infinite regress in Takhoma cannot be disproved by unaided reason.]

* * *

What we must give greater attention is how the child's unique kind of imagining contributes to the full temporal life of faith. We are in a better position to do this today because of recent explorations in the psychoanalytic sciences.

The following few observations are based on the work of writers in England of the quality of D. W. Winnicott (*Playing and Reality*), Charles Rycroft (*Imagination and Reality*), and Marion Milner (*On Not Being Able to Paint*).[4] I shall turn their work to my account but, I think, not with distortion.

First I borrow from Charles Rycroft a summary of

this development which he does not hesitate to describe as perhaps the most outstanding contribution to psychoanalytic theory in the last thirty years.

Psychoanalytic theory, he proposes, has always presented us classically with two realms of experience, one psychical and subjective, located within the self, the other environmental, objective, located in the world. The first is in inherent opposition to the latter, to external reality; the task of life is to surrender the omnipotence of the first principle and to adjust to the reality of the second.

But now we begin to explore a third transitional or intermediate area of experience. It is the area of childhood illusion (which I shall choose to call the faith and believing of this stage). (1) In it the subjective and the objective are fused (what I wish is what is, what I imagine is what is). (2) In it there are two functions; the one is wish-fulfilling, the other is adaptive to reality. *"To the extent that this illusion is successfully created and premature disillusionment is avoided, the individual will feel at home in the world and have a creative relationship with it"* (italics mine).[5] This surely means that someone is willing to play the game of belief with the child. But to my mind all this is only a sharper, less differentiated, less ironized, less ambivalent version of the problem of every man at every stage of life: how shall he relate his longing for happiness to reality; how shall he prevent an impossible gap between his wishes and the real world, belief and reality. Do the images he has formed help him to contact (cathect) objects happily or is he forced finally to contact only the images (idealization) and to handle reality with all the degrees of hopeless parody and irony.

Successful fusion, on the other hand, leads to freedom from the belief that desire and reality are in inevitable opposition to one another and, in Milner's words, to "the development of a creative relation to the world." I think Milner would agree that this creative relation includes the capacity for ecstatic and joyful experience of external reality [i.e., ecstasy which is not based on manic defense].[6]

*   *   *

This new kind of thinking within the mental sciences—almost within the laboratory itself—seems to me extraordinarily important. It is a decisive step forward in our explorations into the relations between imagination and reality and, if I may pursue my own problem, the relations between faith and experience—for I am finding it easier and easier to equate faith and imagination. The new theorists are modest because they acknowledge that poets like Coleridge and Wordsworth anticipated them by far.

But this third world should, on any consideration, throw into the shade the apparently courageous but finally crude answers of men like R. D. Laing (*The Divided Self*) and others, with their adulation of an isolated madness as solution to all the problems of an isolated universe. This is only another attempt to create another form of Dionysus and to enthrone a sterile madness in the lonely places on the mountains. I doubt if anyone who has ever been mad was not glad to leave that dull and solitudinous state.

But the true dreamer, or the recomposer of reality, is one who dares to forge a new hypothesis and slowly match it to possibility. With all these we are indeed in a third world, a new world, a tight unity of paradigm and fact or faith and fact, a world for which we will never be able to set final limits. It is necessary again to say that it is a quality found as often in the simple man as in the intellectual.

Therefore the legends and the fairy tales, and the parents and friends who cooperate, are building imagination and belief. I do not mean to be careless, or to confuse things that should not be confused. I am still saying that faith is a great aboriginal force, with its own temporal rhythms, that is always growing and being educated. Nor have I neglected all of Freud's classical attacks on neurotic belief—beautifully written attacks in which he is careful to add that he is dealing with the psychology and not the reality of the problem.

*   *   *

What did Christ mean when he said: Unless you become like little children you shall not enter the kingdom of God. Did he mean innocence? Simplicity? Or was he thinking of the child's capacity to believe? Not the capacity to believe anything and everything, but the capacity to believe. We sometimes forget that preeminent among all Christ's own titles is that of the Son of God. He is the Son; God is the Father. He is preoccupied with the thought of God as Father, not for any arbitrary reason but because he is the Son. He is in this relationship from all eternity, and will be. And with an incredible attachment to the same relationship he becomes the Son of Man. And he is the child of the earth: for the earth shall bud forth a savior.

It seems to me that if Christ is the most central image of faith he is also the most bothersome image of faith. For why salvation by Christ? Is this high particularity not arbitrary, and an offense against the religious spirit, and finally a vulgar attack on the glory of all the great archetypes of Salvation? But it is ironical that the glorious general archetype of Salvation (such as the Orphic passage from evil and darkness to purification and light) inclines to miss the point of the *depth* of Salvation. For the new promise given to aboriginal faith is that we are redeemed not into anything or everything, but into being the sons of God. This is the revolution in the history of faith. But there is only one Son and it is by being joined to that sonship that we shall be, not just redeemed, but redeemed to the degree we shall be. An original curse is transformed into Sonship. This was seen by Hosea (1:10), with what fullness of clarity I do not know:

> The number of the children of Israel shall be as the sand of the sea, which cannot be measured or numbered. And it shall come to pass, that in the place where it was said unto them, ye are not my people, there it shall be said unto them, Ye are the sons of the living God.

*   *   *

Why then, when long ago in Spain men and women were enjoying what Erik K. Erikson might call a moratorium of illusory faith before they would enter the world of adulthood, when they were again ready to believe all things, why then did the great Miguel de Cervantes launch his immortal attack (for such, in the half of its purpose, it is), in *Don Quixote,* on all the all-believing and all-concocting romances of chivalry that had preceded his own masterpiece? Was Byron right in saying:

> Cervantes smiled Spain's chivalry away; . . .
> And therefore have his volumes done such harm,
> That all their glory, as a composition,
> Was dearly purchased by his land's perdition.[7]

Cervantes, I gather on the other hand, was not so much composing a fiction as giving a social sketch of a substantial amount of Spanish reading, dreaming, and actual feeling when he wrote his very early description of Don Quixote:

> . . . he so buried himself in his books that he spent the nights reading from dawn till daybreak and the days from dawn till dark; and so from little sleep and much reading, his brain dried up and he lost his wits. He filled his mind with all that he read in them, with enchantments, battles, quarrels, challenges, wounds, wooings, loves, torments and other impossible nonsense; and so deeply did he steep his imagination in the belief that all the fanciful stuff he read was true, that to his mind no history in the world was more authentic. He used to say that the Cid Ruy Diaz must have been a very good knight, but that he could not be compared to the knight of the Burning Sword, who with a single backstroke had cleft a pair of fierce and monstrous giants in two. . . .
> In fact, now that he had utterly wrecked his reason he fell into the strangest fancy that ever a madman had in the whole world. He thought it fit and proper, both in order to increase his renown and to serve the state, to turn knight errant and

travel through the world with horse and armour in search of adventures, following in every way the practice of the knights errant he had read of, redressing all manners of wrongs, and exposing himself to chances and dangers by the overcoming of which he might win eternal honour and renown. Already the poor man fancied himself crowned by the valours of his arm, at least with the empire of Trebizond; and so, carried away by the strange pleasure he derived from these agreeable thoughts, he hastened to translate his desires into action.[8]

And so he rides forth, believing all things and ever since provoking great human laughter. But how strange is the history of this novel. Cervantes can be said to have accomplished his object. He had attacked something that should have been attacked, grown-up people weeping hysterically, with no distinction between their tears and the world, at a wound to a knight or a rejection by his lady, tilting at windmills, turning prostitutes into princesses. It had all left Spain behind advancing civilization. (Buñuel, the brilliant film director, in *The Milky Way,* has just done a fine cinematic version of this strain of the Spanish character. Many critics have solemnly taken the picture as an attack on Christianity, but it is just a lot of Spanish theological fun.) After Cervantes no more such stuff was written; even the old things were no longer published; it was one of the many significant moments in the education of faith.

But who shall say that it did not also advance the dialogue between the paradigm and the fact, imagination and reality, faith and the world, to a new level? In the end the mad Don Quixote and the realistic servant Sancho Panza have moved much closer to each other than in the satiric beginnings of the story. The knight has grown down; the servant has grown up, they love each other, as these two parts in us should.

It is part of the march of faith, not an abstract epiphany, but a human rhythm. Don Quixote is a giant step forward in this dialogue between the two parts of ourselves. It is a giant step beyond the murderous dialogue between Dionysus and Pentheus. I should like to see the English analysts extend their new studies in this direction and in these more expansive terms.

*   *   *

There is a fascination about all the younger forms of faith and their ecstasies. We can hardly remember the first forms, but they must have been surrounded, for security's sake, by a world of dreams and frequent unalloyed happiness, or at least the longing for the perfect thing. The English philosopher John Macmurray suggests that the child can wait only because of the regularity of satisfaction and the temporal surety of expectation. The expected, that thing in which the child has faith, is not yet coming in the form of the unexpected. The giver, the promiser, the mother, at this stage of things, dare not yet give anything but the expected though she must soon begin to be the teacher of its opposite. There is not yet present that part of faith which we can call the ironic imagination—the part which, creatively even if with suffering, will later be able to put the expected and the unexpected together under the single but variable images of faith. Now, instead, faith responds to any variation with univocal rage. And being doubly afraid, because of its fear of its rage, it will not yet stand for any variation in its univocal images. It dreams, but its dreams have no relationship to history and do not take their birth from history. Not yet. The choices are still beauty and rage. This is Dionysus, beauty and rage.

2. The Unexpected

Now we approach a second stage.

The hypothesis we are exploring is the hypothesis of faith as a great primal human force that in its beginning is as yet indeterminate and is antecedent to all thought and to all verification. Perhaps we can say that it comes into force (which is better than saying that it comes into being) as soon as promises begin to be made to it. These promises need not always be spoken. I have said that most of the fundamental forms of faith are carved without words into the very structures of nature. The womb of the mother is a promise to the child. From earliest childhood faith becomes an increasingly active dialogue with promise. It is almost a dance of gestures between the mother and the child, a dance of offer, response, increasing complexity, testing, verification, misplacements, anticipations, overdemands, joys, cries, screams, withdrawals, renewals. There are so many steady, verified promises that there is the law of God: Honor thy father and thy mother. They are the makers and executors of promise.

One important part of the life of faith is the testing of the promises made to us, whether by the mother or the world or Christ. A promise is made to faith and faith looks for or discovers or composes evidence for the promise. As and if it takes the promise more seriously it will become more and more sensitive to finding evidence; just as the good man finds the good, so faith finds evidence. Or again, certain things that might be or once were evidence against the promise are now no longer taken as such. It will be easier to understand how faith is thus placed at the interior of the evidence if we propose to ourselves that faith has its own epistemology. The latter is now about to set out on a long development, not without suffering.

Let me give a partial description and example of this epistemology of faith. For one thing it is a very fascinating combination of the sense of the expected and the sense of the unexpected. A promise made to faith leads one to *expect*. God enters into a covenant with Abraham, telling him the great things he shall *expect* (your descendants shall be as the sands of the sea). Expectations, therefore (and the keeping of the image of what is promised before the mind), is one of the most powerful forces in man and in faith. The other element of an educated faith is the sense of the unexpected. You must slay Isaac, your only son. How to keep these two things together, without them destroying each other, is the half of life and the whole of faith. Now too we are moving toward our irony. It is only by keeping the expected and the unexpected together in an irony of a definite character that faith is able to compose and recompose evidence according to its own epistemology. To learn to recompose is the heart of its education.

Even as the whole history of the Jews, the child is now moving into a world of opposites, a world where he must begin, in faith, to master the coexistence of the expected and the unexpected and where ecstasy meets its opposites. In Dionysus this moment produced overwhelming hatred. In the Christian it must be mastered by irony. But by the irony of Christ. It seems a long road. And, necessarily, the details are always changing. The details are always contemporaneous, to put it mildly.

*   *   *

God promises something in the Scriptures, but what is promised in one event again and again becomes clear only when the predicted event happens. The unexpected has intervened, forcing us to return to the original promise to understand it anew. The prophets, from Moses to John the Baptist, are always relating promises and present. The present is a piece of evidence that is now inserted into the former picture.

The coming of Christ is seen in the light of the expected, is expected by the imagination as the latter lives within a given series of historical events. But the coming of Christ had not been, had never been, expected in this form. The coming of the kingdom had been expected, but not in the form in which it appears in and is described by Christ. The ironies of Christ had not been expected.

*   *   *

It is the Jews who more than all of us in our day have had to face the problem of the unexpected within the heart of the universe and to calculate the nature of faith accordingly. It is as though, more than any others, they have been forced to go down into that very abyss of the irrational which Pascal so awfully forced upon the Enlightenment and the modern intelligence. No people has been asked to face more. One Jewish thinker puts the modern Jewish plight about faith in the following way:

Strangely enough, for we would expect the opposite, he tells us that there was a complete collapse of the death-of-God movement in the Jewish community. And within that community there was no philosophic furor concerning how to speak about God such as that raised among Protestants by Paul Van Buren or by Leslie Dewart among Catholics. The crisis of belief among the Jews came instead from the question of God in History. "The Holocaust under Hitler could somehow be ignored by Christian scholars talking about the reality of God, but for Jews it was the central problem. Auschwitz and all the other death camps became an unanswerable protest against God's goodness or His very existence."[9]

Here it is, but where is it, the irrational? I listen to these noble words, and I know that we are in the presence of muted words, of minds muted in the presence of numbers like six million. We talk of nude bodies, strips of skin left, the gold in the teeth gone, the hair calculated and gone, the ring, the leather skin, the pain that yields only to endless fatigue, to look at one's neighbors in this hell beyond hell. We read of a few men who have survived this, able at all cost to call themselves human yet and not to yield to the inhuman. No wonder the mind returns to a single lonely scene—perhaps of a suffering child such as Dostoevski pictured in *The Brothers Karamazov*—rather than yield to the sleep of these numbers. A certain modesty of the imagination recoils even at the individual scene and dares to call it a hysterical scene. And then six million is a hysterical number. The problem of belief becomes strangely double for the imagination. On the surface the problem of faith is: how to believe in God and that much good? But apparently the imagination has difficulty in believing in this much evil. In either case, in the individual case of Dostoevski's child it declares that the author's imagination is extreme; in the group case, in the case of the six million, it fades, through convenient grouping, into unbelief. The number remains, but the imagination, not being really able to consent, has canceled it.

For the Jews the temptation against faith could not have been more obvious. But if such horror on the part of men should lead to a protest against the universe and God and a denial of his existence, then the horror would be even worse. For if the universe has no use for man, or for meaning and value, how can we stand up against it? "Without God there is no reason to be righteously indignant about anything men do.... Though Hitler could not succeed in putting an end to Jewry, we would now be doing that for him" if we ceased to believe.[10]

And why be angry? For if there is no God then Auschwitz has as much right to be and is as true as anything else.

*   *   *

The gap I wish to mention next is precisely the opposite of the gap suffered by Job or the Jews. It the gap between the expected and unexpected as it is found between the death and the resurrection of Christ. It is the gap between the two images of our own death and our own resurrection. As we bury someone close to us it is the distance between the forlorn fact and the possibility. What it comes down to is the gap created by the good news itself, between things as we see them and the incredible promise. If a substance of irony be precisely defined by the nature of the distance between co-existing elements in life or in art, then we cannot image a greater irony than the Christian.

It would be absurd to say that the news of the resurrection and the promise of eternal life creates suffering. This form of the unexpected creates joy, of course. Still the very size of the joy and the gap does create more than one problem that comes near to suffering. One would think that in the presence of great joy one would be in the presence of a passive situation where the promise would overwhelm the will. But I do not think faith works that way. The process, for faith and the imagination, is still active. What seems to be required of us is a certain energy, without which we cannot move ourselves toward the image of the promise.

Let me put this in another way. We wait for faith to descend from above, and so it does. But it *has* descended from above. We who believe have it. Yet we continue to wait for it to appear from above. It takes, literally, *energy* to dare to raise the images of faith in the imagination. Apparently even the images of the good and of happiness can become too much and too overwhelming for mankind, especially where men are overcome by negative images of themselves and do not have the moral energy to lift themselves to any form of brightness. So that even the joyful must be mastered and must be approached with mastery of it. We will see later that it is something in the present and in our actual humanity of the moment, some good taste of the self, as it is now, no matter how small the taste, that will help bridge the gap between the actual and the promise. In

some form or other the kingdom of God must be
already there, or else the mind will not take the step
from the actual to the possible. It is especially the
mentally ill who find it almost impossible to expect, or
to believe they have a right to do so.

It is necessary to educate ourselves to endure the
unexpected. But it is a terrible thing not to be able to
expect. Thus again it is necessary to keep together, in
one struggling act of the imagination, the expected and
the unexpected. The child had learned to expect. All the
life of the city of man is based on this expectation, on
what we can expect of each other, at home, in school, in
traffic, everywhere. The movement of the muscles, the
dance of our walk in a crowd, has expectation built into
it. It is part of what I call the body or the physiology of
faith.

To be able to expect seems both to require and to
create energy.

*   *   *

There were a number of central elements of the
Christian declaration of what henceforth could be expected which prevented it from becoming an elite doctrine to be taught in secret to elite groups. Principal
among these were the basic ironies of the new teaching.
The Gospel of Jesus Christ, his full and complex declara-
tions, were not given to the rich or the talented; on the
contrary, we were told how difficult it would be for a
rich man to enter the kingdom of heaven. Not only was
the good news to be preached especially to the poor,
but poverty and death, the very final qualities of all
human nature, were declared to be the permanent ironic

modes leading to their opposites of salvation and well-being. Part therefore of the announcement of the resurrection was that it had come after a complete passage through our humanity and through a real death. Thus the good news was located, as we shall see, at the center of our humanity, in such a way that any ideological or intellectual takeover of the announcement was, over any great time, impossible. This could not but lead, in time, to a development of confidence in himself on the part of the ordinary man. It made the news completely public, something to pass on in public speech and flame, as in the scene in Athens and the other great cities of the East when, at midnight on Holy Saturday, the whole word is suddenly ablaze with candles and with the public cry and greeting: Christ is truly risen. So that the joy was not private but intensified by this public and open quality. But at the same time this fundamental irony of salvation through the human prevented, indeed negated, hysteria. For one had to remain human at any cost, and to die in order to rise from the dead.

3. Building a Present Moment

Now faith is stepping more and more deeply not into the timeless but into time. Above all, it must build an actual present.

I would like to make one or two more brief explorations of the creative relationship of the present to faith and to the future promised by faith.

Very often an idea is better understood when we know, with a fair degree of clarity, what its opposite is. Let me follow this methodology here.

What I am concerned to develop is the creative force

exercised by the present on the capacity, the energy, of faith to believe in its own promises. Let us now imagine a present that is empty and bare, that has no good taste at all. The kind of images of the future produced by *such* a present is exactly the reverse of the images of faith. The images become apocalyptic in the most negative sense. Where we now indulge in every manner of negative image of ourselves changed by every wind, the rages that result can generate not only images of the end of the world but of ourselves in violence doing the ending. A mean image begets a mean image. The imagination becomes frightened at its own negative power. It is easy now to believe in the dead. In fact, situation after situation, bad enough in itself, reaches, in fantasy, the degree of the diabolical.

This is where we are today in our imagining of reality. There is no limit to our faith in this kind of imagined world, no limit to this ironic view. Literally, it is a fantastic irony, flooded by fantasy, accompanied by a reverse energy and a deep joy of its own. It imitates faith in every way, in energizing, in believing, in projecting a future. But its irony is unique to itself. It is a corrupt image of faith. For what it now does to the present is the reverse of the actions of hope and faith and Christic irony. It returns to the idea of any present action and laughs it to scorn. It does not build a present; it destroys whatever remnants of a present are left. It mocks at any idea of action, much less ordinary action by ordinary people. It falls back on spectacular action supported by more apocalyptic fantasy. And if the whole process is nowhere supported by the good taste of self and the achievement of the realistic imagination, the back and forth cycle between helplessness and apoc-

alyptic images moves into endless escalation. The fantasies harden into fact. The fantasies of this destructive
version ironize all action out of existence. It becomes
fashionable not to act or to live. This is what I call
negative faith, and this is its irony. It is not an image of
faith. Its magnificence is a cheap imitation of the real
thing.

*   *   *

One philosopher tells us that, after all, there is only
one time and that is the present. All other times are to
be defined in terms of the present. The present *is*. The
past is that which once was, which was once in the state
of being or *is,* but no longer is. The future is that which
shall be, but *is* not yet.

This is not to create a movement or an ideological
point of time out of the present. For the present becomes completely present to itself (which, if there is
always *only* a present, remains the only thing that
matters) by the help of the past and the future.

One looks back upon the past in order rightly to read,
imagine, and compose the present. This is what Moses,
as first great interpreter and prophet, did with the
Jewish people in the book of Deuteronomy. This is
what Christ did with the disciples on the road to Emmaus after his passion and resurrection. We look back
on our past to see the turns and windings, to remember
all the times of impossibility when there was no way
out; no one but ourselves can read with accuracy the
mirabilia dei, the marvelous ways of God.

The future is looked to as world of promise and
possibility, but it is the present that is, then, not only
fact but fact and possibility. The whole canon of the

Old Testament is alive with possibility, promise, expectation.

The imagination can steal its structure from this story and can learn to be in the presence of that which is and is not yet, never separating the two, never rejecting the present but creating it, by the help of what was and what shall be. In this sense, in this sense with substance, there is only the present, and there is only the detail of the present. But it is exactly detail and articulated line which is the task of the imagination. We let Christ give us an image of the present.

*   *   *

This power of the present to create the future, and not a minimizing of the future, may be something of what is meant by Christ in those many passages where he seems to be commanding faith to live in the present and not in the future.

I bid you therefore not to fret about your lives, and what to eat and drink; nor about your bodies, and what to put on them. Is not life more than food, and the body more than clothing? Look at the birds of the sky. They neither sow nor reap, nor bring the harvest into barns; and yet your Heavenly Father feeds them. Are you not of greater consequence than they?

"Can any one of you by fretting add a moment to his years? Then why be troubled about clothes? Learn from the lilies in the fields and how they grow. They do not work, they do not spin. But I tell you that not even Solomon in all his glory was robed like one of these. And if God so clothes the grass of the fields, which is there today and thrown into the oven tomorrow, will he not all the more clothe you, slow though you are to trust him?

"Then do not fret and say, 'What are we going to eat or drink?' or 'What will there be for us to wear?'—things that the pagan world pursues—for your Heavenly Father knows that all these things are your necessities. No; pursue the Kingdom and God's goodness first, and these things too will all be yours.

"Do not then be anxious about tomorrow, for tomorrow will look after itself. Today's trouble is enough for today."[11]

* * *

When we move into the present, we are moving through time. We are also letting actual time move us and, as it were, do some of the work.

Among the recollections of Auschwitz by Primo Levi, author of *If This Is a Man* and *The Truce,* there is the following description of a friend and his faith:

. . . after only one week of prison, the instinct for cleanliness completely disappeared in me. I wander aimlessly around the washroom when I suddenly see Steinlauf, my friend aged almost fifty, with nude torso, scrub his neck and shoulders with little success (he has no soap) but great energy. Steinlauf sees me and greets me, and without preamble asks me severely why I do not wash. Why should I wash? Would I be better off than I am? Would I please someone more? Would I live a day, an hour longer? I would probably live a shorter time because to wash is an effort, a waste of energy and warmth. . . . We will all die, we are all about to die . . . Steinlauf interrupts me. He has finished washing and is now drying himself with his cloth jacket which he was holding before wrapped up between his knees and which he will soon put on. And without interrupting the operation he administers me a complete lesson. . . . This was the sense, not forgotten either then or later: that precisely because the Lager was a great machine to reduce us to beasts, we must not become beasts; that even in this place one can survive, to tell the story, to bear witness; and that to survive we must force ourselves to save at least the skeleton, the scaffolding, the form of civilization. . . . We must walk erect, without dragging our feet, not in homage to Prussian discipline but to remain alive, not to begin to die.[12]

*   *   *

Not only does the theology of hope, as it is now constituted, think in a preoccupied and one-dimensional way about the future. I have the further impression that when it observes someone emphasizing the importance of the present then the theorist of the present is imagined to be doing precisely the same thing, thinking in an absolute way about the present moment. Just mention the word (the present) and the philosophical fantasies begin to rise as overwhelming ghosts. Jürgen Moltmann's *The Theology of Hope* is a beautiful and valuable book but let Pascal be heard mentioning this word of ours ("So we never live, but we hope to live; and, as we are always preparing to be happy, it is inevitable we should never be so") and at once the theologian descends upon him.[13] What does the word about the present mean?

Nothing short of being "Always the protest against the Christian hope and against the transcendental consciousness resulting from it. . . ." Then an unfortunate sentence about the present from Goethe ("All is always present in it. Past and future it does not know"); another from Hegel; then Nietzsche; but as climax there is the grand figure of Parmenides, the permanent bête-noire of the theology of the God of promise and the future. For Parmenides reality was not only one single, present tense ("The unity that is being never was, never will be, for now it is all at once as a whole" [Frg. 8, Diels]); it does not allow for division, or change, or passage, or coming to be, or any kind of difference. This of course is an image of the present which excludes any possibility of a future, of a not-yet, of possibility, of a promise.

There is, then, in much of the theology of hope a distrust of talk about the present and a magnificent picture of a hope and a future that alone makes any present possible or livable. God himself is a God of the future.

But I believe in promise in terms of this already done.

*   *   *

It is precisely this part of the epistemology of belief that is neglected and omitted by the theologians of the new theology of hope. The more one reacts in this new theological development the more one becomes aware not so much of their creative relationship to a creative image of the future, of possibility, of promises—for that is indeed a contribution—but of a preoccupying and almost obsessional concern with a hope anchored in the future. Their future and their hope, that which is moved toward, is what gives life to the present, and the energy to act in the present. But this position, even for the sake of hope, is too simplistic and does not, I repeat, take sufficient account of the complex way in which human life moves along the lines of time. It does not take account of the way in which the present creates the future or communicates the energy to maintain the images of promise. Nor does it sufficiently emphasize the role played by the memory of the past in helping us maintain the promises. There was an almost violent unexpectedness, so far as the promises were concerned, in the life, death, and resurrection of Jesus Christ, but on the road to Emmaus it was the promises and texts of the past that he called upon to explain his death and resurrection.

But whether in the case of past or present what we are now talking about is more than a matter of prophecy or metaphor or typology of the future. Both past and present have their own life and actuality in a history: they are themselves achievements. Like a mother (the keeper of promises to her child) they anchor the imagination in the midst of promises already achieved or a kingdom already being lived in. In the case of the Jews of the twentieth century I have used the metaphor and reality of their humanity, and any fraction thereof, not because I wish to reduce the promises to the shape of the human as we know it but because it will always be the human as we know it that will be redeemed. Therefore it was actual present flesh that had to be asserted and washed.

I keep returning to today's revolutionary not out of a spirit of negation but because I am interested. More often than not the contemporary revolutionary rejects all the past. He ought, instead, to pick his ancestor. And name, even in a fumbling way, his future. Thus he will avoid the deception of the totalitarian revolutionary, who refuses to name his program or his future. This is the principal criticism lodged against the totalitarian imagination and revolution by Hannah Arendt in *The Origins of Totalitarianism.* [14]

*   *   *

It is understandable, then, that Freud expresses himself very strongly and very negatively in the presence of the question of "the meaning of life." For certainly the question of the meaning of life (and the possibility of faith) is often asked by those who have difficulty in finding meaning in the present. Because this is so, both faith and hope have developed a bad name by giving the impression that they belong to the life of fantasy rather than to the realistic imagination. Things can go so that they generate wild dreams and unfounded hopes. The fantasy is only an outward picture of an inward ill, the acting out of inward things, a kind of picturing of something ill. On the social scale the picture and the painting and the images become more monumental and more violent. Long histories of such pictures of hope and faith are given to us by Norman Cohn in his *The Pursuit of the Millennium,* pictures of monumental but hallucinated hopes of whole peoples who have been diseased by poverty and abandonment. The exhausted traveler in the desert, without water, sees water everywhere. The inner longing, on and on and on, for a letter, makes us see a letter in any form of light or white in a box. The conflicts on the outside of a man are often only shadows cast by an interior battle. Freud, knowing much more, clinically, about this kind of interior life, concluded it was *this* kind of life that generated the question of the meaning of life. He thought it came from a diseased present moment; he puts it thus, in a letter to Marie Bonaparte:

> The moment a man questions the meaning and value of life he is sick. . . . By asking this question one is merely admitting to a store of unsatisfied libido to which something else must have happened, a kind of fermentation leading to sadness and depression.[15]

What shape does the image of faith take here? It is the image of something born of a loss of contact with the present; it is a substitute, in the order of fantasy, a picture of this failure. It is a dream born of sadness. If it were seen rightly it is a form of mourning for a dead dream.

*   *   *

Once again, therefore, I do not see that it is a very good idea to say: What good is it to do anything if there is no resurrection? For this makes the resurrection seem to be only a hope of desperation. It would be better that the resurrection was an image of divine reality believed in by men close to earthly reality and capable of handling it. But the insertion into the present, without sadness or depression, is also a constant questioner of the meaning of life, without sadness or depression. Only in this case it is more an assertion and an assent than a question. It is also the back and forth, back and forth, between the whole and the part, between the faith in the moment and the faith in life.

Now, therefore, I pick up my courage to say, in my

own dialogue with the revolutionary: stop using the scapegoat of the bourgeoisie and the middle class to disguise any inability of your own to live in the present or build a house or take a sleep. The proletariat never did become the revolution but instead became a very wide middle class; the Negro revolutionary is faced with the problem that his own people is becoming a middle class; the poor wish to become members; the intellectuals are members, with guilt, of the middle class. The whole discussion is a cliché, hiding the fact that we do not yet know what is the real problem. So far as daring and conservatism go the present situation is curiously confusing. For it is the most middle class of the old vocabulary who want to go to the moon, and beyond and beyond. But it is the revolutionary who on many counts is the new conservative and who, knowing that something is profoundly wrong—that is certain—and thinking he has the answer, decides he is bored by the journey to the moon and by this whole great moment in the history of the human spirit. What is his language? It is the language, *mutatis mutandis,* of the old religious fundamentalism, a curious mixture of the apocalyptic and a real touch of spiritual genius that does not yet know how to prophesy. But he thinks that apart from complex history he can look for and declare the single prophecy.

* * *

I have introduced the name of Freud and have spoken of him as a man who believed that our image of the future and our image of hope depends upon our feeling and taste for the present. But on that score it may be more important to speak about Marx and Marxism. Is it not true that the strongest assault on religious faith in modern history has been brought by Karl Marx? But that assault was based on the proposal that religion and religious faith was a *perversion* of the thus-far failure of civilization to create a present with truly human economic structures; because man in his work is presently alienated from his humanity he creates an image of faith in a future, an image which would be needless, which would not even have occurred to the imagination if we had a better world. It is our unhappy state in the economic present which projects the state of happiness in the future. But what we are ourselves exploring in this section is the possibility that the holding on to some fundamental grip on our present humanity, with no matter how meagre a grip, is precisely the thing that helps us most to hold onto our images of faith.

But one way or other, whether seeming to move for or against images of faith, the dimension of the present has become a far more critical dimension for faith than ever before. It may be the proddings of the two great figures of Freud and Marx that have pushed the man of faith more decisively into this arena. What they are in a position to do, armed as they can be with a more fully dramatic image of time, with memory, and with hope, is to create a mightier, not a weaker, image of the present. The problem of the present has become, not absolute of course, but crucially important for modern theology.

*   *   *

The importance of the present and of detail is why some of the Jews in the prison camps fought to the very end to keep some scrap, even the smallest, of their humanity. They washed themselves and kept themselves in some smallest fraction of trim even when there was no sense at all in doing so. It was not that they kept to some last vestige of a hygienic civilization. Judgment of these things must vary in every concrete situation. In this situation it was to hold on to the last vestige of their humanity so that something could come out of it. And I am suggesting that if this were held onto it would be more possible to believe.

*   *   *

But now let me translate the phrase "the last vestige of their humanity" of my previous thought so that it reads: "the last vestige of their faith." For when you want to take away the last vestige of a man's humanity you must strike at the last vestige of faith in him. If we would read or reread George Orwell's *1984* we would have to agree that that is the final subject and insight of the novel. The lone man and the lone woman rebel against the absolute state and their rebellion takes the form of their forbidden love of each other. There is something left, some fine scrap left of their humanity, until they are forced to betray each other and the last taste of faith has been destroyed on earth. Then all real feeling for the present vanishes completely and it becomes impossible to hope.

4. The Movement through Infinite Possibility

There is nothing that modern sensibility is more aware of than that it has moved into a world of infinite possibility.

The new range of possibility exists both on the inside and the outside of man. There are not only the new vistas of space and time. There are new infinites, new open worlds, that emerge on the very inside of man. As an example of what I mean I think of our infinite freedom as we confront the beginnings of the new world of the genetic engineering of mankind and the determination of the very shape of the human by the new biology. Soon, if not already, individually, nationally, internationally, we shall be allowing and forbidding ourselves possibilities of human development; we shall be much more in charge of the *free* advance of evolution than ever before. I will suggest a fine article-bibliography on this subject which has been discovered for me by my good friend and neighbor, the Jesuit biologist Jerome Gruszczyk: Thomas R. Mertens and Sandra R. Robinson, "Selected Readings in Genetic Engineering," in *The American Biology Teacher,* May, 1973, pp. 282-286. There is also an issue of *Theological Studies* (September 1972) that is completely devoted to the subject and that is eminently valuable. And my thoughts go back again to that extraordinary section "The Fear of Freedom" in Dodds's *The Greeks and the Irrational:* Dodds describes for us a situation in which, at least once before, an ascendant human culture, faced with new magnitudes of possibility and a new freedom, turned instead in fright into the paths of superstitious passions and irrelevant imitations of a true idea of revolution.

I want by all means to avoid apocalyptic language because it is very pretentious and, fortunately, has thus far been always wrong. But is it too much to say that no generations as much as ours have been asked to deal with the problem of infinite possibility and to work out those images which will enable us to cope with it? What, here, are the images of faith?

We are by now far removed from childhood images of faith. But the child's vast images are flooding us in suddenly real and unexpected forms.

Also we are beginning to come full circle in this book to the point at which we originally set up our confrontation between the image of the world as it was viewed by the writers of the York dramatic manuscript and the enormous modern line of unimaginable space and time and possibility. Here the subject is so vast that I can only offer a few very limited thoughts for meditation. I shall be especially interested in those overly rational and Euclidean images of God and the world which have so often blocked the development in us of better and more coping images of faith. And I shall be thinking doubly of infinite possibility, as something to be bound and as something to enjoy.

*   *   *

What does rationalism mean when it asks: What is the meaning of everything? What does faith mean when it asks the same question? Surely the image God has of the world is not a rational, "well-ordered" image. Faith which has learned to deal with the unexpected, with irony, relieves the imagination (and the emotional life) of the burden of such images. And these rational images are a very great burden for the imagination if they turn out to be impossible or unreal. They drive one to think and to think, and to imagine and imagine, in an endless and ineffective way. True, it is the whole burden of these pages that faith is a place of thought; it thinks and must think. But only the rationalistic assumption of some perfect plan, pattern, order and reason will make it think and think without end or without rest, seeking a kind of answer that is not there for every situation and for life itself. A perfectly rational God would have limits. But a God who can tolerate and suffer so much freedom, so many free people (plus so many who are not free!), so many interesting, conflicting freedoms, so much time, so much waiting, so much evil and hatred that has no reason, so much space and time, does not have these limits. Yet it is the lack of system in the system that leads men to say there is no God. When the systematic fails they say he is silent or dead.

This is what Dostoevski might be saying—it might even be what he is having Ivan say—in that memorable conversation in the *The Brothers Karamazov* in which Ivan challenges Alyosha's God for having created a world in which innocent children can suffer so terribly. He tells the story of the consequences for a child after he threw a stone in play and hurt the paw of a certain general's favorite hound. The child is stripped naked before all the hounds in full hunting parade and in the presence of his mother. He shivers, cold with terror. He is ordered to run. The hounds are after him and tear him to pieces before his mother's eyes.

Shall we say that this is part of a symphonic harmony? Ivan cannot endure such an image of faith; why should he?

*   *   *

Ivan Karamazov now declares, after his storytelling, that it is his Euclidean understanding of the universe that causes all the difficulties. Nor can he stand an explanation of evil that is based on reaching some future final harmony. For in this future final harmony this child will still have been torn to pieces by the hounds and by this monster.

The assumption of the precise intellectual thing called liberalism in contemporary thought is that if we manage to build a perfect social system, these things will not happen and all will be well. Certainly we must keep trying to do this, we must try without end, but it is only a certain faith in the added factor of the incomprehensible that will prevent the building of the systematic from being completely poisoned by the very political fanaticisms and hatreds and despairs we are trying to eliminate. If liberalism could tolerate chaos, and deal with it a little more ironically, it could handle it better.

In a totalitarian world infinite possibility is excluded. For how could the image be tolerated? Security would be threatened. Thus too, and for the same reason, the free and creative imagination is excluded, is an enemy.

*   *   *

Says Ivan Karamazov:

> With my pitiful, earthly, Euclidean under-
> standing, all I know is that there is suffering and
> that there are none guilty; that cause follows
> effect, simply and directly; that everything flows
> and finds its level—but that's only Euclidean non-
> sense. I know that, and I can't consent to live by it.
> What comfort is it to me that there are none guilty
> and that cause follows effect simply and directly,
> and that I know it—I must have justice, or I will

destroy myself. And not justice in some remote infinite time and space, but here on earth, and that I could see myself. I have believed in it. I want to see it, and if I am dead by then, let me rise again, for if it all happens without me, it will be too unfair. Surely I haven't suffered, simply that I, my crimes and my sufferings, may manure the soil of the future harmony for somebody else.[16]

I can again agree with Ivan that these images of symphony and evolutionary harmony are not images of faith. But why did this happen to the child. I don't know. And that is a better image of faith.

*   *   *

We must ask ourselves what we are saying when we say that faith sees a final harmony and order behind it all (in which everything finally works out). But in many senses everything finally does *not* work out. The sheer evil that will have been so multiply done will remain done and evil. Of course there is also incredible order and harmony in the universe. But there is also incredible disorder, and the point I am and will be making is that perhaps God emerges incredibly greater for "going ahead anyway with it all" on these and not other terms.

The distinguished theologian John Hick has written to the contrary. He thinks that within unlimited time all men will finally choose the good, and thus a final perfect victory of the good: " . . . it is also morally and practically certain that in unlimited time, in a universe ruled by a love that is actively seeking their deepest good, each will come into harmony with the divine ground of his own being."[17]

I cannot help but think that behind this sentiment lies the conviction that everything must work out if God's goodness and omnipotence are to be safeguarded. Nor can I dismiss the thought that finally Ivan Karamazov may be more right than John Hick. I myself am more overwhelmed by the image of a God who is not overcome by so much complexity over the whole vast stretch of time, so much evil, absurdity, confusion. We must guard against a simplistic understanding of the phrase: everything turns out for the best. For there are many senses in which this is simply not true. It is not for the best that *this* man were born. "It were better for this man that he had never been born."

* * *

We must also explore the question whether or not the traditional and sacrosanct idea of God that has been given to us by a long line of Christian philosophers working within the vocabulary of Aristotle is not itself part of the problem of the overly rational images of faith. If God is only immutable (and not also mutable), if we are indeed really related to God but not he really to us, if the action of God in history produces no history in God, if all the sorrow of this world does not produce an affection within an all-perfect God, if nothing we do can add to the fullness of Being, then we are dealing with a God who satisfies the needs of a very distinctive rationality but cannot be said to satisfy the needs of biblical reality or human feeling.

These are a few parallel sentences from Joseph Donceel in his essay "Second Thoughts on the Nature of God":

] 150 [

If God remains immutable whether he creates or does not create, then the whole of creation makes no difference to him. The eons of evolution, the millennia of human struggle, the drama and tragedy of human history, all the travail of man's civilization, leave God totally unaffected in his Olympian immutability. In final analysis, this whole gigantic endeavor has no real value, since it adds nothing and can add nothing whatsoever to the eternal fullness of being which is God.[18]

* * *

We have moved into the middle of the life of the images of faith. There is wrestling involved.

If we follow the imagination of the monk in *Rashomon* (the great picture of the Japanese director Kurosawa), we can see how his whole personality is struggling to get into the images he is forming or that are coming at him. He realizes, I suggest, that if he does not get into them, and deeply into them, he is lost or will be destroyed. Let us conceive the action of the picture in this way, under the assumption, that is to say, that the picture is all about him. In one way or another the whole action passes through him and it is he who must keep the pieces together, with some judgment, with patience, with strength, with compassion, but not with denial, or perish.

The story, on the surface, is simple. A woman is raped, and her husband murdered. The woman tells her story. The attacking bandit tells his story. So does the observing peasant. So does the shade of the murdered man. Everything contradicts everything else. The differences, the lies, the contradictory interests, the possible betrayals of everybody by everybody else, pour into the heart of the monk. It is he—and we with him—who must struggle with faith and in faith and come out somehow with an image of it all that will mean his own interpreting survival, his own not-corrupting, noncorrupted action. It must be that he suffers. Every grown man and woman does this struggling with images every day of their lives. Faith moves into serenity and the forging of one of its images, but it must not accept the burden of starting with serenity. Faith is a moving, and a wrestling. Look, says Ivan K., what the universe did to Christ.

*   *   *

Surely there is an intensely important way in which a God in the middle of history reacting to everything in history remains the same. He is corrupted by nothing and surrenders his identity or his thoughts to nothing. His thoughts remain not our thoughts. The light he throws on everything comes from the center of himself. It is as though he were the universal image for the good man who living in the world does not lose his soul. And he is the paradigm for the definition of religion itself in the Epistle of St. James: "To visit the sick and to keep oneself unspotted from this world."

There is a type of irony—it is often called romantic irony—in which the writer remains conscious of all the contradictions of life, finally remains completely conscious, free and detached. The writer is God. The work at its " 'lower' level is a game—a cat-and-mouse game with mice that the cat is really fascinated by and quite attached to. To the reader, whom the author takes into his confidence, the work has become a spectacle to observe with detached amusement as well as a story to be absorbed by; it is now one and now the other. . . ."[19]

How different, in every possible taste, from the image and the irony of the God of the Old Testament. And the New. He is always Lord and master but never amused, entertained, or detached. Christ settled that.

*   *   *

With some of the writers of the West, then, the idea of infinite possibility has become a kind of infinite ironic smile on the part of God (and on the part of the writer!). So Heine in his *Confessions:*

> Alas, the irony of God weighs heavily upon me. The Great Author of the universe, the Aristophanes of heaven, wished to show me—the little, earthly, so-called German Aristophanes—as glaringly as possible what feeble little jests my most bitter sarcasms were in comparison with his own, and how inferior I was to him in humour and in giant wit.[20]

This image of irony is deep in the mood of the modern intelligence, again preventing it from a real affection for the more miserable parts of itself and the world. But it comes as more of a shock to find it in James Joyce, who could perhaps say it more easily in a theory like the following from *A Portrait of the Artist as a Young Man* than when writing the great soliloquy of Molly Bloom:

> The Artist, like the God of Creation, remains within or behind or beyond or above his hand-

work, refined out of existence, indifferent, paring his finger nails.[21]

As an image of faith imagine Christ paring his fingernails.

* * *

We are within the movement into infinite possibility. How can I deal with infinite possibility?

This leads to the question of what we might call the internalizing of Providence. First we must determine what is meant by the question: "Can we internalize Providence?" I begin by rejecting any notion that internalizing Providence, in my use of it, means *psychologizing* Providence: that it means the elimination of the existence of God and of the objectivity of the whole question. Nevertheless it certainly does mean the insertion of an important and corresponding element of subjectivity into the picture. Struggling for the proper form of the question (much has to be known or felt before we can ask the proper form of a question) we put it this way: Can we control the infinite possibility, the infinite risk of the world, by what finite action we take and by what we are in the very internal structure of our souls? The two elements within Providence, of objectivity and subjectivity, come together in the sentence. "To those who love God all things worketh unto good." Can we therefore go so far as to say that faith in God is not only faith in a Providence but is itself an internalizing of Providence, in the sense that faith keeps infinite possibility under control and directs it? For one thing, since faith and the love of God have no taste for evil they will have no commerce with it, will instinctively avoid it. We who have some love of evil will always find it.

*　　*　　*

That which is selected most distinctively by Hannah Arendt (in *The Human Condition*) as able to control the infinite dark of infinite possibility and the infinite future is the idea of promise.[22] That is why it is so fatuous to say that vows should not be made, for who can foretell the future, and who knows how he or she will feel five years from now. One of the most completely human things about me is that I have ways of setting many endings to many forms of endlessness and that I can *choose* to know how I will feel five years from now. I decide to elaborate my identity not only into the past but into the future as well. But between my doing so and not doing so, there is infinite space. Thus, at least in one way, I control the infinite irony of the universe.

The limitation of infinite possibility is the promises of God, the covenants of God.

A covenant is a solemn pact or treaty of promise and response. Let us remember the four great covenants or promises of God with the human race. There is the covenant with Noe, the second with Abraham (repeated with Isaac and Jacob), the third with Moses and the people of Israel, and the last, in perpetuity, with the New Testament in Jesus Christ.

Here is a binding of infinite possibility but not of the unexpected. For faith knows that the promises will be kept, but in what form it does not know.

*　　*　　*

] 155 [

Thus promise and Providence are two of the great personal forces which bind the world of infinite possibility. But that is only half of the question and only deals with the large lines of infinite possibility as it may be danger or threat to the smaller lines of man, threatening to dissolve or destroy him or reduce him to an unsubstantial shadow. The other half of the matter is the joy of infinite possibility, of change, of hope, and of the new. It is this positive image of endlessness that is an image of faith and that must give joy to science and the imagination.

5. The Passage through the Curse

Now we must pass through the stage of successfully imagining *the curse* or what seems to be the curse. Though it is better to say that this difficult task is the work of a lifetime. It is that large a task for our images to move, or keep moving, from darkness into light.

I shall first of all put down what I conceive to be the three principal factors we deal with when we deal with the curse. Then I shall cite what are probably the two most important scriptural texts.

It is easy to note the precise identity of the three factors, but their relationship will prove to be quite difficult. They are: (1) There has been a curse upon the human race and upon the earth. (2) That curse exists no more because the Son of God took upon himself the curse, on the cross, and was blessed for it in the resurrection. (3) But all the consequences and children of the curse remain: above all, there is death; there is sorrow, suffering of body and mind, all the ills that flesh is heir to, separation, misunderstanding, ill repute, grief and mourning, poverty, weakness, mental illness, war perhaps without end. But these things are not a curse. In fact many of the things that were once a curse are now numbered among the beatitudes, the things that are blessed (by the irony of faith the curse is blessing). Nevertheless, they are, to put it mildly, facts and are to be treated that way by the imagination.

*   *   *

Here are the two texts, one from the third chapter of Genesis, the other from the third chapter of the Epistle of St. Paul to the Galatians:

> Unto the woman he said, I will greatly multiply thy sorrow and thy conception; in sorrow thou shalt bring forth children; and thy desire shall be to thy husband, and he shall rule over thee.
>
> And unto Adam he said: because you listened to the voice of your wife and ate from the tree of which I had forbidden you to eat, accursed be the soil because of you. With suffering shall you get your food from it every day of your life. It shall yield you brambles and thistles, and you shall eat wild plants. With sweat on your brow shall you eat your bread, until you return to the soil as you were taken from it. For dust you are and to dust you shall return. [Gen. 3:16-19]
>
> Christ redeemed us from the curse of the Law by being cursed for our sake, since scripture says: Cursed be everyone who is hanged upon a tree. This was done so that in Christ Jesus the blessing

of Abraham might include the pagans, and so through faith we might receive the promised Spirit. [Gal. 3:13-14]

*   *   *

What is our image of the curse and its consequences?

Nothing is more difficult for the imagination than to make a successful composition of all the elements of curse and consequences (there has been a curse; there is now no curse; the consequences of the curse remain; the consequences are by irony turned into blessing), but nothing is more crucial.

I will first make brief mention of four critical passages through the curse, three vast ways in which it has been or is being imaged, and shall then try to give quick elaboration.

1. There was the paradigmatic and activating passage of Christ through curse and through death and all its companionship. Such is Christ's doing and imagining—of the curse, of the separation from the Father ("My God, my God, why hast thou forsaken me?"), of the love of the Father, the weakness, the death—that he receives the redemptive acceptance of the resurrection and the cancellation of the curse.

2. But this paradigm was never meant to act univocally or with pure externality. We take the help of the paradigm to make our own passage and our own image. Each imagination must make the passage, as Christ did, from darkness into the light of the new image. But never into the kind of light, or transformation of the images, that removes the consequences or terms of the ancient curse. The story is different in every life, but the con-

sequences—the sorrow, pain, death—are always there, as is the central task, by help of irony, for the transforming imagination. Faith's final image of the curse is forged by a co-passage through the life of Christ and through human form, human limit, and the live consequences of the dead curse.

3. But there is vast evidence that the national imagination is in danger of completely reversing the fundamental directions of this passage of the imagination. I shall not yet enlarge the matter: we hide or deny or romanticize the consequences of the curse, preferring not even to speak of them, or choosing to create a passionate solution based on an absolute utopianism in politics; on the other hand we are nationally obsessed with a sense of the curse and its accompanying guilt, an obsession that has its own kind of joy. This raises the possibility that the more we deny the consequences of the curse the more we restore the terrible influence of the powerful memories of the dead curse.

4. There is the vast world of mental illness, and within this world the effects of the sense of the curse, together with its inability to cope with the consequences through the healing images of irony.

*   *   *

Here is the way I put things to myself for our present now and state. The redemption is there but must be received and imagined. But what is also there are all the powerful and sorrowful elements of the curse, without now being curse. There is the poverty, the sorrow, the death, all the haunting images of separation and alienation. Pascal says yes but Rousseau still says no, there is no curse, past or present, there is only the history of the curse of the political order. Change the political; then our dreams, our images, will become beautiful and our nightmares will go.

On the surface this generates a quarrel between the men of faith and those who believe in the political solution. Because this surface dichotomy was given its head we have witnessed the great polarity between religion and Marxism and the separation, again and again, of the religious consciousness from the history of social revolution.

But over the long term it may not and must not be so. The conditions of the curse remain, but this only deepens the ironic image—for the promises are achieved through the very conditions of the curse.

The images of faith are redemptive, personally and politically.

One of the major qualities of the irony of the images and faith is that it is redemptive. For let us consider again. On the one hand there are the superb and royal promises of faith. On the other hand they are related to and achieved in their opposites, in the human and in weakness. This is the central irony. The promises are especially made to the very poor, the weak, the suffering, the oppressed. What I wish to say a second time is that this irony has an internal and an external aspect, the two being deeply related. It is to the weak and human parts of me, the man that is sick and shall die, that the promises are made and the revelation is given. I participate in the redemption of Christ by transforming the images of these parts in me, this weakness and this death. They have been under a curse, and faith, if it is not to lose its nerve, must continue, in its own images, to declare that curse, even more clearly than literature, which has been trying to seize hold of it on the profound terms of Homer, Sophocles ("It is better that a man should never have been born, or if born to depart this life as soon as possible"), Shakespeare, Dostoevski.

Christ placed himself under that curse and embraced all it meant. He seems to have tasted it to the full. It should be easier for those who accept the consequences of the curse and who do not throw these weak, suffering parts of themselves into the exterior darkness of contempt and disgust but approach their own poverty and death with redemptive, affectionate images—it should be easier for them to objectify and universalize this curse, to refuse, above all, to accept the terrible dichotomy between the rich and poor nations, and in the best sense to become completely "political" in their devotion to Asia, Africa, Latin America. In other words their ironic image of themselves should become politically productive. But if they hate both the curse and themselves, if they cannot lead their illness and poverty back into the human order, much less the divine, they will not really be able to stand the sight of all those who in the external order represent the curse. The poor have their own way of sensing this and will refuse their own communion to those who are so unironic about themselves and who think the poor are cursed.

*　　　*　　　*

So the stages of life are also the stages of our images of the curse. It is surely not the work of a moment, or of a sudden epiphany, but the work of a lifetime, and of a movement into the future to rewrite the past, before men convert the image of the curse into the image of the blessing. To believe in *this* irony is precisely faith.

It is always a matter, ironically, of keeping the two situations, the curse and the conditions of the curse, together in the right way. And of course this is most difficult. It was in fact so difficult for the Jews themselves that as one solution of contrary promises many of them developed a double tradition of the Messiah and resolutely kept the two images separated: there was the image of Messiah ben David, the victorious king, and Messiah ben Joseph, the sufferer.

* * *

How to imagine the curse? At a certain point, when the fatigue of the world sets in, this becomes the question.

But here I am, for myself, at one of the centers of discussion for this whole book. Here the crucial question is how to imagine the curse. We need a history and extra information to imagine it rightly, and there is nothing more important in human life than to be able to do that, no matter how small the approximation or the success. I repeat: All the sorrow of the curse is there, and all the realism. But not the curse. To what extent does this make possible the transformation of our images. The danger is a priority and a religiosity that denies the reality of the world. This has been the meaning often given to faith's transformation of the images and that situation leads many people to say "transformation be damned," to turn away in derision, and to fall back completely on the writers and the artists alone for some closer sense of the truth.

On the other hand we have but to look at the frequent forms taken by mental illness to see what comes into existence where men and women are seized, without *any* transformation, by the sense of the curse, and self-punishment: mistakes, failure, sickness, game legs, national adversity, and death itself cannot be seen in the double light that they are terrible but all right. How often does the modern theologian preach the end of the curse? What is needed is some, any escape, not from the facts, but from some endlessly dark abysmal prison of the imagination, where the patient is always hastening, legalistically, because of the curse, being sure of God's thoughts, to punish himself before God does. My own country seems especially vulnerable not to vast waves of mental illness but to wave upon wave of a self-laceration that often seems beyond satisfaction.

Notice again an outrageous paradox going on that certainly needs some correction of the images. All in all the images threaten now to stand on their head. On the one hand there is a good deal of denial of the actual effects of the curse, a refusal, for example, to imagine death and a marvelous dedication to the beauty of Dionysus, in a word a rejection of the facts; on the other hand this is accompanied by unlimited statements of reveling in the curse itself, an enormous brooding of the imagination, an excommunication of all those who will not join this new church and the new image of faith. I repeat my hypothesis: Perhaps it is the very inability to imagine the facts and the history of the curse directly that causes this vague and uncontrolled outbreak of the curse in every crevy, corner, and depth of the imagination. It is ironic that the very means taken to repress the curse always gives it new life.

So the images go in pairs, but never ironic pairs, never with ironic self-awareness. All would be beautiful if we did the right thing, but there is an enormous curse upon us, we are an accursed tribe. We are a beautiful people, but we are surrounded by the worst, the very worst of times. There is in the air both things, a denial of mortality and a terrible sense of apocalypse. The curse, the end, is near. If you are cheerful, you do not belong, you are mad. The intellectuals, enjoying the curse, look knowingly at each other and whisper their cabalistic secret: this is the worst of times, this is the worst of times. The irony becomes glib, almost corrupt. The beautiful people gloat in the curse.

6. The Tragic

Let us move into the tragic, large or small.

The next question is the question of the tragic. I want to think of those coexisting contraries, faith and the tragic. Now must the Son of Man go up unto Jerusalem.

A prevailing image of faith is that it is not and cannot be tragic. It is not and cannot be tragic, the assumption is, because we know that everything finally works out and is finally a harmony, without an unsuccessful note. The Christian knows that in the end he will rise from the dead, to a perfect justice within which there will be a correction of all evil and a re-adjudication of all inequalities.

The ultimate and magnificent summary of this image is drawn from the final pages of the Apocalypse of St. John. I am so enamoured of these images of the Apocalypse that I took myself once, by happy fortune, to the island of Patmos, at the eastern end of the Aegean sea, and read them all in the cave where John is said to have composed them. This is the ultimate image:

> Then I saw a new heaven and a new earth, for the first heaven and the first earth had vanished, and there was no longer any sea. I saw the holy city, new Jerusalem, coming down out of heaven from God, made ready like a bride adorned for her husband. I heard a loud voice proclaiming from the throne. 'Now at last God has his dwelling among men! He will dwell among them and they shall be his people, and God himself will be with them. He will wipe every tear from their eyes; there shall be an end to death, and to mourning and crying and pain; for the old order has passed away!'
>
> Then he who sat on the throne said, 'Behold! I am making all things new! (And he said to me, 'Write this down; for these words are trustworthy and true. Indeed they are already fulfilled.') 'I am the Alpha and the Omega, the beginning and the end. A draught from the water-springs of life will be my free gift to the thirsty. All this is the victor's heritage; and I will be his God and he shall be my son. But as for the cowardly, the faithless, and the vile, murderers, fornicators, sorcerers, idolaters, and liars of every kind, their lot will be the second death, in the lake that burns with sulphurous flames.'[23]

The question is: with such an ending in view, how can the images of faith be tragic?

*　　*　　*

Tragedy and *the tragic* are most certainly difficult words to define. In the long history of the imagination and the sets of images that have been de facto associated with them we move through a very wide range of sensibility. Therefore, any single and simplistic image of the tragic is bound to omit many sovereignly tragic moments and feelings that have occurred in history and literature. That being taken for granted, I wish to take the risk of delimiting a certain part of the spectrum of these images that has been of central and constant occurrence as men have thought and lived the tragic.

I take death itself, both as a fact and as a metaphor, to be the central subject of tragedy. By death I mean what the hospitals mean; it is a complete helplessness; it is a chasm of helplessness; it is, like tragedy itself, the passage from being able to do something to being able to do nothing. As a fact this is true in the fullest physical sense. As a metaphor, it means all those analogous passages of the human spirit into what resembles death, into all the recognition of all the forms of the mortalities of human sensibility: failure, shame, the recognition of mortality, the coming to a truth that is the dropping of a mask, the coming into the range of human pain, sorrow, and solitude. As a metaphor it is an irony, for it means the revelation that life and honor hide their opposites, as does the beauty that we know.

To say that all this is absent from the world of faith is to do faith itself a profound injustice. And yet we have often done it that injustice and communicated to it easy victories, easy graces which have done it no good. It has sometimes been as though, having penetrated with great insight and compassion into the sorrowful world of Shakespeare, we must then prove textually that he also had a Christian view of life (and death). But faith does not remove death or its passage into helplessness, the end of energy, and the reaching of a kind of deep nothingness. It is the grace to give in to this ending, this weakness, this nothingness, that seems to mark the peace and the difference that faith is after. Faith does not alter the facts or alter the structures of the human. Far from killing or dissolving the tragic, faith seems to take it as its own special territory, affirming it, confirming it, amplifying it, extending it, deepening it, in order precisely to accomplish its own special objectives. Above all, it sticks unalterably to the facts. If it dissolved the facts, what good would it be? The facts would still be there.

We make no mistake in saying that whatever the other factors death has, it has this to-be-contended-with factor of absolute nothingness at its center. If it is true that we know nothing about it, at least we know it as nothing. Christians are in a position to talk about it as a beginning, but this very position often leads us to romanticize death as not really an end. This, apparently, leads us into the same psychological difficulties about death as it does the man without faith. It is as though the word had gone round that a Christian does not really die, does not really come to an end, does not come, most important of all, to a state of complete helplessness where there is a form of nothing.

I therefore hypothesize that the dead man can do nothing, absolutely nothing. This perception is often inadvertently blocked, not only by the Christian statement that death is a beginning, but also by the Aristotelian image of immortality; the philosophic version too has prevented the full view of this point of absolute nothingness in death and has created the image of a soul still struggling within its own dead but energetic resources to find God in the dark.

We have struggled in many ways against such a full image of death because we really think that there is something wrong with such a taste of the absolute point of nothingness. Therefore we modify or alleviate the image. Whereas the truth is that we must not modify but must give in completely, to the point where there is truly nothing left. This may be the point where love and death are cousins, in that they must know how to give up completely. This may be why the orgastic act of love was in earlier English called *to die.* And that relationship between the two situations is what is being dealt with by John Donne in "The Dreame."

> Perchance as torches which must ready bee,
> Men light and put out, so thou deal'st with mee,
> Thou cam'st to kindle, goest to come; Then I
> Will dreame that hope againe, but else would die.

It is a strange thing that we have to go to the very opposite end of the pole to look for an approximation to the absolute ending and non-being of death. So that the act of love as a fullness is one of the few things that can really describe the emptiness of death—it is so absolute, and such a void, and requires so much passage.

Irony can go no further.

7. Death and Nothingness

Christian irony struggles with its own part of the problem of non-being; it has remained faithful to the fact that there is a point of absolute non-being in man which can be called death. It has not wavered from seeing this fact as a fact. It is this fundamental methodology of fidelity to fact which accounts for the consistency and brilliance of its vision as it has gone on from there.

It could have compromised or temporized with this fact. It must have been tempted often to declare that the man was only half dead, or that the moment of death was really a magnificent and most energetic moment, rather than a moment of complete impotence. But the results would have been disastrous. For men would then be burdened with the hopeless project of not really dying. And they would not have been permitted to submit to it.

Contrarily, what actually happened was that this point of complete impotence, and all its parallel points, became the supremely productive area in man.

For example, the image of faith says that God seems attracted toward the point of non-knowing in man, toward the point of the impotence of the mind. This point is not destroyed or taken away by faith, but used. It is always there, but in such a way, apparently, that it also creates its very opposite.

Hope has the same structure. It does not impose the romantic burden of perpetual human strength. For this is a hopeless project, and hopeless projects are the cause of hopelessness. In hope the weakness, or the impotence, need never go and is always there as instrument for the creation of its opposite. Thus hope does not lead to denial or to fraudulence. It stays with the facts, with all the hospital facts, and does not impose the duty of "overcoming" the facts. What a job that would be: to go around overcoming facts. The truth seems to lie more in the direction of a co-presence of weakness and its opposite. At the furthest point of this way of looking at things absolute non-being comes into the presence of its opposite. At irony's point of complete victory it loses.

*　　*　　*

We talk about the ironic relationship of weakness to power and to salvation. But is is essential that I should not romanticize. Faith's imagination must be a realistic imagination. The weakness we are talking about is an actual weakness. If I really move through all the stages of man and of faith, it is actual aging and old age that I move through. The bones will really ache. I will really feel aches and pains. I will suddenly begin to see that there are old people in the world, moving slowly, with different enabling paces of trying to get somewhere. They have always been with us, but we never saw them. Their fatigue is very deep. They have passed through many points of mourning and grief, grief for the disappearance and death of beautiful image after image of themselves. It is a strange and unexpected creation, and a strange image, for faith to pass through. But it is a fact. The old sometimes wonder if they will have the strength to pass through the weakness. The image they have is of the actuality of the whole process. The young do not know they are there. But there is no curse, there is no curse in age. There is nothing wrong with it. This seems a terribly simplistic thing to say. But it must be said. In our ironic, unironic civilization the old are hardly there. Dionysus has cast them out. The irony of Dionysus is external, melodramatic, and full of hatred.

*　　*　　*

How again to imagine nothingness?

Nothingness is still our most haunting modern problem. Of course it has been wrestled with, intellectually, by men like Hegel, Heidegger, Sartre. But with us it is a wider phenomenon than that which simply haunts the philosophic head. It has gone a big step further and seized hold of the contemporary imagination as one of the latter's principal preoccupations.

It is as though many of our writers are increasingly imagining a vast ocean of nothingness, contingency, or absurdity that underlies things; as though things might lapse back into that ocean if we did not keep a firm grip on some few parts of a great void with their routine or talk; or they hold on to another human being as possibly the last listening ear in the universe; or they try to convince themselves that something actually has happened in the great void; or they wait for the endless time of death.

There is, in this contemporary imagination, a good deal of stripping the world down nearer to the edge of nothingness, so that nothingness should stand no longer hidden.

Camus says, in *The Rebel,* that he would hold on to hell itself rather than nothing.

> In default of inexhaustible happiness, eternal suffering would at least give us a destiny. But we do not even have that consolation, and our worst agonies come to an end one day. One morning, after many dark nights of despair, an irrepressible longing to live will announce to us the fact that all is finished and that suffering has no more meaning than happiness.[24]

But while this is painful and affecting rhetoric it does

] 171 [

not truly imagine "nothing," after the manner of a Beckett, who can find out and reveal the bare bones of things. Fortunately we have much evidence for a new willingness of the imagination to imagine the nothingness of things; it seems to be willing to move up to it as far as possible, and to move into it. The imagination seems able to face a kind of descent into hell, a descent which involves putting off much of the trappings of things. The subject that preoccupies Beckett, he tells us, is that of impotence and failure.[25]

I wonder again if what happens here in Christian faith is not the building of an image of nothingness based on the most final of all ironies: death becomes the final nothing, the final weakness and the final childhood, but it becomes enormously productive in the hands of God. Faith, first of all, has been one of the great driving forces in building up the ironies of this world, from the ordinary to the most extraordinary kind. Again and again we come back to the point that the modern consciousness is indeed ironic, and so is faith. Both faith and modernism deal so much with the passage, the reduction of things to nothing. That is why the modern does not like rhetoric. It senses the hollowness, the noise, in the thing even before it starts. It does not like classicism because it is more preoccupied with the chaos behind the order. When Thomas Mann uses a classical style and tone and set of images in *Death in Venice*, it is only to mock it: for it is only a shocking way of filtering into consciousness the growing images of disgust, rot, passion, disease, death. So it is with our search for beauty. The search, where it exists, is ironic in its intentions. It is only a threshold or a trap, or a mode of ironic laughter, because the thing that is going to emerge is its very opposite. The artist seems to be after beauty but he is after a larger game, the vast ocean of nothingness, a veritable plague that is eating into the beauty. That is what is happening, for example, in *Death in Venice* and in *The Plague* of Camus. It is the constant nature of irony that the game and the intention of the artist turn out to be larger than expected.

* * *

It is not the degree of nothingness behind the ironic image that is the problem. What matters is the kind and the taste of the image we come through with. We always seek an approach to the right irony. One can go only halfway toward the nothingness and the irony, and yet be wild with the rage and the disgust of it. Or one can go not one step, not one single small brave step toward it, staying in the midst of the new beauty that is untainted by the plague underneath the city of Venice, and the result, finally, can be the same. The dream breaks down, the disappointment grows without end, the rage moves in and in and in. Men curse what seems a curse. Or one can go all the way into the nothingness, so that literally nothing is left but death, and yet the taste may turn out differently. I am not thinking yet of the afterlife, because that must yet be another moment and another matter. Faith involves this absolute death and passage through tragic weakness. It is not that it is less tragic than these other approaches. It must be more tragic.

* * *

I keep saying that it is the image and the taste of this

] 173 [

nothingness that seems for faith to be the central thing. Faith never reaches it, but tries for the right taste. We never reach the perfect image of faith. What the right sense or taste means, as in so many things, is the elimination or reduction of the wrong tastes and the wrong senses. It is wrong to say that the right taste is horror, it is not the horror of the concentration camps and what happened there within the bodies of the Jews. For the true horror there was what human monsters could do to human beings. The true taste and the true image cannot be the sweet sickly love of death of the decadent romantics that has been commemorated for us by Mario Praz in *The Romantic Agony*. It is not the rage against life of a poet like Sylvia Plath; yet why, to avoid these things, do we say that at this point our image of faith is not tragic. For man is the only finite being in this world who knows what finiteness is, what a high mountain and a deep depth, what a fact it is, a finitess in that limit. To whom should faith yield in imagining this ending as really ending?

*   *   *

When faith is young and absolute and uneducated as yet by its own developing ironies, it is completely vulnerable. The first years of faith are an inevitable mixture of power (the power of these feelings is clearly overwhelming) and weakness (where is there greater weakness, so completely dependent on this one external figure). Later on, in death, the terms of faith will again be the same. There will be the repetition of the same complete helplessness, only deeper and more complete, as though the original childhood had been but a suggestion and a weak metaphor; there will be the same dependence on one figure, this time to overcome our death and rise again; there will be nothing we, children, can do, so that there is clearly an extraordinary relationship between faith and dependence. These are two different forms of human childhood, birth and death. In each case infancy is an image of faith. "Unless you become as little children you shall not enter the kingdom of heaven." Birth and death have faith carved into them. But in between is the need of the development, in forms both subtle and simple, of what I am calling irony. Not any irony but the irony of faith. The irony of Christ.

But, that I may end where I began, the irony of Christ is Christ himself.

Notes

NOTES TO CHAPTER 1

1. *Christ and Prometheus: A New Image of the Secular* (Notre Dame, Ind.: University of Notre Dame Press, 1970).
2. John Wisdom, "Gods," in Antony Flew, ed., *Logic and Language,* 1st ser. (London: Blackwell, 1951).
3. (Chicago: University of Chicago Press, 1970).
4. (Cambridge: At the University Press, 1958), p. 5. There are other books dealing with parallel views on this subject by S. Körner, *Conceptual Thinking* (Cambridge: University of Bristol, 1955); S. Toulmin, *Foresight and Understanding* (Bloomington: Indiana University Press, 1961); Karl Popper, *Objective Knowledge, an Evolutionary Approach* (Oxford, 1972); W. Sellars, *Science, Perception and Reality* (New York: Humanities Press, 1963).
5. E. K. Chambers, *The Medieval Stage* (Oxford: Clarendon Press, 1903), vol. 2, appendix X, pp. 410-411.
6. Toulmin and Goodfield (New York: Harper, 1965); Koyré (Baltimore: Johns Hopkins, 1957); Von Weizsäcker (London: Routledge, 1952).
7. Robert B. Eckhardt, "Population Genetics and Human Origins," *Scientific American* 226, no. 1 (January, 1972), 94-103. See periods sketch, p. 97.
8. The phrase from Yeats occurs in the short but powerful and prophetic poem "The Second Coming." He is referring to the vast waves of anarchy and evil that he thinks are flooding and will flood human civilization and he is predicting that the center of culture will not hold. There are two ironic moments in the poem: (1) the title; (2) the last two lines ("And what rough beast, its hour come round at last, / Slouches toward Bethlehem to be born?") give surface suggestions of the second coming of a Savior, but they are really talking of the

coming of a vast principle of evil. See Richard Ellman, *The Man and the Masks* (London: Faber and Faber, 1969), pp. 235-237.

9. Mann, *Joseph and His Brothers,* trans. H. T. Lowe-Porter (New York: Knopf, 1938), p. 205.

NOTES TO CHAPTER 2

1. *Medea,* lines 1078-1080, trans. Rex Warner.

2. Aristotle's *Poetics,* trans. S. H. Butcher (New York: Dramabooks, 1961), p. 79.

3. Farnell, *The Cults of the Greek States,* 5 vols. (Oxford, 1896-1909). Dodds, *The Greeks and the Irrational* (Berkeley and Los Angeles: University of California Press, 1951); *Euripides Bacchae,* 2nd ed. (Oxford, at the Clarendon Press, 1960). John Edwin Sandys, *The Bacchae of Euripides* (Cambridge, at the University Press, 1880). Gilbert Norwood *Essays on Euripidean Drama* (Toronto: University of Toronto Press, 1954). A. W. Verrall, *Bacchantes of Euripides* (Cambridge: Cambridge University Press, 1910); *Euripides the Rationalist* (New York: Russell, 1967 repr. of 1895 ed.). R. P. Winnington-Ingram, *Eurpides and Dionysus* (Cambridge: Cambridge University Press, 1948). Gilbert Murray, *Euripides and His Age,* 2nd ed. (Oxford, 1965); Murray, trans., *Bacchae* (Oxford, 1904).

4. Farnell, vol. 5, pp. 85 and 89.

5. (New York: Knopf, 1963), p. 29.

6. (Chicago, 1972), p. 28.

7. *A General Introduction to Psychoanalysis* (New York, 1966), p. 453.

8. Guardini, *The Life of Faith* (Glen Rock, N.J., 1963), p. 87.

9. Thucydides, *History of the Peloponnesian War,* trans. Rex Warner (London: Penguin, n.d.), book 3, chapter 5.

NOTES TO CHAPTER 3

1. Ian T. Ramsey, ed., *Words About God* (New York: Harper, 1971), pp. 202-223.

2. Pascal, *Pensées,* trans. A. J. Krailsheimer (London: Penguin, n.d.), pp. 64 and 66.

3. Cohn (London, 1957; rev. ed., 1970); Knox (New York: Oxford University Press, 1950).

4. Gerard Siegwalt, "La foi-confiance de Luther," *Christus* 18 (June, 1971), 335-343.

5. Auerbach, *Mimesis: The Representation of Reality in Western Literature,* trans. W. R. Trask (Princeton, N.J.: Princeton University Press, 1953), pp. 22, 43.

6. Chapter IV, "Comedy," in my *Christ and Apollo* (New York: New American Library, Mentor-Omega, 1963), pp. 99-117. See especially p. 106 ff.

7. Herbert Marcuse, *One-Dimensional Man* (Boston: Beacon, 1964), p. 123.

8. Ibid., p. 132.

9. Brinton, *The Anatomy of Revolution,* rev. ed. (New York: Prentice Hall, 1952).

NOTES TO CHAPTER 4

1. René A. Spitz, "Anaclitic Depression" in *The Psychoanalytic Study of the Child* (New York: International Universities Press, 1947) 2: 314-315.

2. F. J. Harvey Darton, *Children's Books in England, Five Centuries of Social Life,* 2nd ed. (Cambridge, 1958), p. 297.

3. (Westwood, Mass.: Faxton, 1926).

4. Winnicott (New York: Basic Books, 1971); Rycroft (New York: International Universities Press, 1968); Milner, 2nd rev. ed. (New York: International Universities Press, 1967).

5. Rycroft, *Imagination and Reality,* p. 37.

6. Ibid.

7. *Don Juan,* canto XIII, xi.

8. *Don Quixote,* trans. J. M. Cohen (London: Penguin, n.d.), Part II, chapter 1.

9. Eugene B. Borowitz, "The Postsecular Situation of Jewish Theology," *Theological Studies* 31, no. 3 (September, 1970), 472.

10. Ibid., p. 473.

11. Matt. 6:25-7:3. E. V. Rieu, trans., *The Four Gospels* (London: Penguin, 1952).

12. Quoted by Paul Bailey, "Saving the Scaffolding," *New Statesman,* August 20, 1971, p. 245.

13. *The Theology of Hope* (New York: Harper, 1967), pp. 26-30.

14. (New York: Harcourt, 1966).

15. Quoted by Paul Edwards in the article "Life, Meaning and Value of," in *The Encyclopedia of Philosophy* 4: 477, from *Letters of Sigmund Freud,* trans. James Stern and Tania Stern, ed. E. L. Freud (New York, 1960), p. 438.

16. Dostoevski, *The Brothers Karamazov,* trans. Constance Garnett (New York: Vintage, 1950), p. 289.

17. John Hick, "The Problem of Evil in the First and Last Things," *Journal of Theological Studies,* n.s. 19 (October, 1968), 591-602.

18. *Thought* 46 (1971), 347.

19. D. C. Muecke, *Irony* (London: Methuen, 1970), p. 78.

20. *Confessions,* 1854; quoted by Muecke, *Irony,* p. 39, from *The Poetry and Prose of Heinrich Heine,* ed. and trans. Frederick Ewen (New York, 1948), p. 489.

21. Quoted by Muecke, *Irony,* p. 39, from *A Portrait of the Artist as a Young Man* (London, 1950), p. 245.

22. Arendt, *The Human Condition* (Chicago: University of Chicago Press, 1958). p. 244.

23. Apoc. 21:1-8 (*New English Bible* trans.).

24. *The Rebel* (New York, 1967), p. 261.

25. Cf. particularly Samuel Beckett, *Proust and Three Dialogues* (London, 1965), p. 125ff.

Index